Looking Up, Looking In

Building Emotionally Intelligent Leadership Habits

Graham Andrewartha

16pt

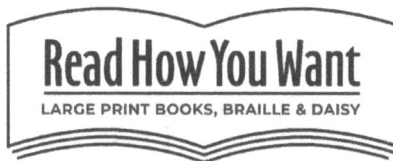

Read How You Want

LARGE PRINT BOOKS, BRAILLE & DAISY

Copyright Page from the Original Book

TABLE OF CONTENTS

'You extend the most generous interpretation possible to the intentions, words, and actions of others.'
~Brené Brown

PRAISE FOR LOOKING UP, LOOKING IN

"Over nearly 40 years I have had the pleasure of working with some truly wise leaders. Common to all were attributes such as self-awareness, courage, candour, and respect. Each also had the ability to engage their emotions, whether to connect, create or strategise. Leading in this way fostered trust, that which builds bridges across siloed structures and minds, and creates an enabling environment that allows people to flourish. The ability to look up, out and in is often confronting, but always enriching. Graham's book, Looking Up, Looking In, examines some of the key qualities which allow us to do so, but then he goes on to tie them to the skills involved in influential leadership practice. In doing so he offers the reader a practical guideline for reflecting on the first, and building on the second, on their journey along their leadership path."

~Dr Fiona Kerr, Founder and Director, The NeuroTech Institute

"Looking Up, Looking In is a practical, very real and motivating MUST read. Graham's insights and advice have led to renewed self-reflection on how I function in life generally but also how I lead my family and staff working in my businesses. More importantly, this book offers direction on how to improve my shortcomings. We are all WIP and no more so than when we head up organisations. This guiding book has assisted me and will assist you, to be better, do better and become a more empathetic and effective person in life and as a business leader. A strongly recommended read!"

~Ennio J Mercuri, Managing Director,
Ennio Group of Companies

"*Looking In, Looking Up* gives you the tools to make changes in the way you interact with people to improve your relationship with them. It inspires you to want to make those changes to gain that better outcome."

~Richard Maurovic, artist, 2001 Federal
Government Centenary Medal,
1997 South Australian Citizen of the year

"Leadership isn't just about a training course – it takes commitment to change. In *Looking Up, Looking In*, Graham brings his decades of experience as both a psychologist and leadership coach to provide a practical pathway to changing beliefs and behaviours that hold us back from being better leaders."

~Sean Lloyd, International strategy and risk expert

"This is an excellent book full of well researched insights. It is a must read for current

and aspiring leaders or anyone who seeks to improve their impact with others. It is full of practical and easily applied guidance and tools."
~Danielle Jiranek, General Manager People and Culture, Beyond Bank

"*Looking Up, Looking In* gives us a great, easy-to-use roadmap for becoming more effective leaders. You'll enjoy the real-life examples and practical steps you can put to use with your team and your family today!"
~Pete Walsh, Master Coach, Peak Workout Business Coaching, Arizona

"*Looking Up, Looking In* is part of a new movement to transform leadership and personal development. The scary fact is that most leadership development programs do not effectively develop leaders. One of the primary reasons for this is that these programs have largely ignored the part of leader that controls how a leader processes and operates: the mind. The absence of the mind in leadership development is largely due to the fact that until 2005 we didn't know much about the mind of a leader. Fortunately, since 2005, we have learned more about the mind than all of time before that. This is now leading to transformational books like this that finally integrate the mind into leadership development. Thus, if you want to

practice cutting-edge leadership and personal development ideas, this book is for you."
~Ryan Gottfredson PhD, Leadership Professor and Wall Street Journal best-selling author of *Success Mindsets*

FOREWORD

If a conductor of an orchestra wants a perfect concert, she brings out the music inside each musician.

If a comedienne wants to prompt someone to laugh, she offers a joke.

If a football coach wants a winning game, he elicits the excitement in each player.

But how would you elicit the realisation of leadership?

Just like in the first three examples, the idea is to offer an experience that orients toward the attainable target. A simple example: To elicit leadership, you might assign a task like giving a tour, that would require an individual to lead rather than follow.

Why do we need to orient toward in these cases rather than offering someone information? Because a concept is best realised by experience, not by absorbing information. In such cases the target is a by-product of an experience.

Therefore, to prompt a realisation or a concept, evocative communication is needed, not informative communication. Informative communication is used in mathematics and science—when there is something to compute and the result will be concrete. For example, when summing the cardinal numbers from 1-100, the result will always be 5,050. Similarly, in physics, the equation F=ma explains the concrete relationship between force, mass, and acceleration.

But if the target is the conceptual realisation of leadership and its concomitant state and identity, then it would take an experience to elicit it. And it might require a series of evocative events that entail experiencing components of leadership, including focus, vision, motivation, connection, responsibility, empathy, and positivity, the sum of which could elicit a synergistic amalgamation that would prompt the realisation of leadership.

And because there is no linear path to leadership and the goal is not concrete, we choose heuristics over an algorithms when communicating this concept. An algorithm is a set of logical steps that leads to a tangible result. A heuristic is a simplifying assumption that targets a realisation, such as leadership or one of its components. And there are since there are many dimensions to leadership, it is intangible and not concrete.

When eliciting a concept like leadership there may be a progression of evocative steps: Idea/Concept/Realisation/Orientation/State/Identity.

Now if someone does not understand what leadership is as an idea, you can offer its definition, but this will not lead to any of the other steps in the progression. To realise any of one of those steps an evocative experience is required. And ideally, a dynamic experience of leadership would eventually prompt someone have a new identity – "I am a leader."

If someone offers you information, it is absorbed in the left hemisphere of the brain. We could call that learning process the "top-down" approach. However, realisations that are elicited through lived experience, could be considered the "bottom-up" approach, where knowledge is not required to understand something.

With *Looking Up, Looking In,* Graham Andrewartha has created the perfect leadership book that can stimulate into play the realisation of leadership. There is a balance between information and case examples and exercises that will prompt realisations. Andrewartha also backs up his propositions with current neurobiological research.

This is a foundational book on leadership written by a renowned and highly respected expert. I passionately recommend it.

Jeffrey K. Zeig, PhD
Founder and Director
The Milton H. Erickson Foundation
Phoenix, Arizona.

PREFACE

On a cold rainy day in 2019, my son phoned me to discuss the idea of writing a book on trust and leadership. By the end of that week I had sent him twenty snippets and articles on the subject that were part of my own reference material collection.

I continued accumulating material and spent a great deal of time reflecting on my client sessions, and our team's work studying neuroscience, brain plasticity, mirroring, and the myriad ways human beings communicate – and don't communicate. I mused on the fact that all of us have multiple conversations, and yet misunderstanding and confusion abound.

Misunderstanding is the default condition. Workplace problems and conflict rarely occur when there has clearly been a misunderstanding. Rather, they occur when we mistakenly think we have understood the other person

Given the large number of leadership programs and books, learning how to communicate as a leader is a really popular theme. In spite of this, we seem to make little progress when it comes to being understood.

As a psychologist I have always known we are human beings first and leaders second. We bring into our work roles the values and drivers and biases that we learnt in our early developing years.

As CEO Julie Michael said, 'I carry many of the values that have been ingrained in me throughout my childhood and bring those to the boardroom.' Of course, we each carry both positive and negative values.

Somehow leadership development forgets this fact and teaches leadership skills as if we have no ingrained personal background in communication practice. Leadership books and courses provide some good leadership skills and techniques whilst ignoring that these skills and techniques are being attached to underlying bedrock values and biases about ourselves and others.

Unless we change those values and biases first, by getting rid of our unhelpful learnt behaviours and expanding our helpful behaviours, then we will never develop influential leadership skills.

With all this in mind, I was inspired to write *Looking Up, Looking In.*

DEDICATION

Looking Up, looking In is for the two Es in my life. My grandkids, Evie and Eddie.

They are intrinsically motivated from within. Their drive and wish to achieve is internal not external (except perhaps for ice cream).

They have abundant energy and curiosity and enjoy learning from making multiple mistakes and errors from which they delightedly learn more about themselves and their world.

They are naturally kind to others except for the occasional tantrum which passes quickly and bears no grudge.

They are my inspiration for great leadership.

I am so grateful to Rick Maurovic my favourite artist and grammar pedant.

He read the manuscript and found every error – except the ones I ignored.

I

WHY THIS BOOK?

'I've learned that people will forget what you said, people will forget what you did, but people will never forget how you made them feel.'
– Maya Angelou

We are swamped with all manner of leadership courses, books, chat shows, and anecdotes, all telling us about the seven different styles of leadership, how management and leadership are different, how Jack Welch or Pinocchio are great leaders, how we should follow the 'Z' method, and on and on. Leadership training is a $360 billion industry in the US, and a recent survey suggested that globally, there are more than 90,000 leadership books and articles published each year. So what is the return on this huge investment?

A recent Gallup poll found that only 18 per cent of managers demonstrate a high level of talent for managing others. This means that a shocking 82 per cent of managers are not very good at leading people.

CEOs are left with a stark choice. Invest in ineffective leadership training with a terrible return on investment (ROI) or cut the training budget altogether. This second option may seem tempting, but the evidence is that doing nothing is just as costly as terrible training.

The costs don't stop with the training, though. The reality is that instead of increasing productivity, ineffective leadership training actually costs organisations around 7 per cent of company sales each year. It also causes untold human suffering.

So, with more than a little irony, here's yet another leadership book!

A NEW APPROACH TO DEVELOPMENT

It seems natural that leadership books focus on leadership development. However, there is a fatal flaw with this approach, and this flaw is the reason why so many books about leadership are ineffective, and even counterproductive.

A leader isn't an abstract thing. A leader is a person. This means any development that takes place needs to be primarily about the person, rather than the role.

As a concept, this sounds straightforward. However, the idea of focusing on personal development, particularly in a professional context, can feel uncomfortable to many business leaders. In fact, developing your *self*, as opposed to developing a *style* is a much more comfortable approach to building your leadership skills. For this reason, we will be exploring how you become a leader who is *you,* not a *type,* such as 'autocratic', 'charismatic', or 'laissez-faire'.

WHAT DOES GOOD LEADERSHIP REQUIRE?

In different situations, every one of us is able to take a leadership role. The *person* you are is the *leader* you are. A good leader uses who they are to create a unique connection with every person they interact with. Even though each leader is an individual, and each connection they make is unique, there are some generalisations that can be made about the skills required for good leadership.

Good leaders require:
- A strong work ethic.
- Resourcefulness.
- Continuous self-improvement.
- Emotional intelligence.
- Adaptability.
- Forgiveness (of themselves and others).

Being a leader means working in a non-ordered world. Workplaces are contradictory and confusing. This means that leaders need to be honest and consistent in order to effectively deal with the endless variety of people they encounter inside and outside their organisation.

As a result, good leaders need to be able to identify numerous personality types and traits quickly and non-judgementally, have the ability to manage their own internal reactions to each of these different personalities, and use the most appropriate method of communication to ensure they are leading effectively.

This requires the ability to match the individual's need with your input. With this in mind, this book intentionally intertwines leadership and personal development.

DO YOU MIND?

Some of the methods outlined in this book will be more appealing to 'you', the leader, than others. However, it is still worth considering those methods and ideas that seem less 'you' because the aim is to improve your leadership skills, not just solidify your current competencies. Throughout the book, there is a strong focus on changing existing neural pathways and creating new ones. Our mind plays such an important role in how we lead, and if we want to improve our leadership, we need to open our minds to new possibilities and new ways of being.

We all think we communicate very well, but few of us do. Even when we have a high level of awareness and experience, there will still be times when we miscommunicate. Communication isn't just speaking. We communicate with our whole body, and our demeanour. A fundamental key to good leadership is learning how to think before you talk. Leadership is a quality, not a position. Having a high-ranking role within an organisation does not necessarily equate to having a good communication style.

We are often sceptical about any evidence that contradicts what we think we 'know'. Therefore, one point to carefully consider is the belief systems we build up, and how we can take a more objective approach in order to enhance our leadership skills.

Another aspect of leadership that we will be looking at is the ability to manage risk. All big project, strategic, and political decisions require an astute leader to see ahead without bias, and to make decisions by balancing risk with safety. Careless risk can result in disaster. Equally, risk-averse safety can lead to obsolescence. Our experiences inform our decision-making, pushing us to risk or resist.

Big consulting firms have increasingly embraced the 'whole brain' concept of training both the analytical left-brain processes and also the right-brain emotional processes. This is largely because strategic planning has taken a nosedive as a money-making part of global consultants' portfolios. Yet they still simplify and underestimate the complexity of how all the bits of our brains work, together and how we are programmed to view reality, going right back to day one of our life on this planet.

We all have cognitive biases. By understanding and overcoming our biases, we can begin to master influential leadership. Developing this ability requires effort and thoughtful application, but it is fun.

CRUCIAL LEADERSHIP, TESTING TIMES

Going back to communication, think about how you approach significant conversations – the ones where you *really, truly* want to be more influential.

This might be putting a proposal to an important client, managing a work crisis, challenging a popular direction for the business, proposing a broad culture change, or admitting you made a mistake.

These significant conversations are often crucial for the wellbeing of the organisation, and for the wellbeing of your own career. If you are effective, you are a star. If you don't succeed, you may never recover.

Leadership is a human process. The vast majority of leadership challenges are human challenges, not technical ones. As a leader, you are your primary asset in any situation. How you show up in a meeting greatly determines the degree of caution or courage, openness or insecurity, trust or wariness, innovative or constricted thinking that is possible.

LEARNING, HABITS, AND THE BRAIN

By engaging in good habits in a consistent way you move beyond needing to build a strategy from scratch every single time. In order to create a solid framework, you need to spend some time exploring the ways you can best retain your learning.

Forming a habit is the key to retaining new information. The best way to achieve this is to make it simple, make it small, make it realistic in terms of your existing commitments, and make it meaningful in the context of your life.

Habits are repeated learned pathways in our brain. First it's a new event. You want to repeat it, so you do – over and over. Then you don't think about it again. It has become integrated into your way of being. All habits, good and bad, have three parts: cue, routine, and reward.

This is called a 'habit loop', which is a neurological pattern that governs any habit. The loop is always started with a cue, a trigger that transfers the brain into a mode that automatically determines which habit to use.[1]

The core of the habit is a mental, emotional, or physical routine. Finally, there is a reward, which helps your brain determine if this particular loop is worth remembering for the future. The cue and reward become neurologically intertwined until a sense of craving emerges.

These two parts of the loop are etched into the brain. This means that in order to change a habit, you keep the initial cue, replace the routine, and keep the reward.

EXAMPLE – CHANGING YOUR HABITS

One habit might be talking to clients about proposals. The cue could be the desire to ensure you secure the contract. Your routine might be anxiety which means you talk too much and too fast, and the reward might be feeling good that you've impressed your client.

To change this example using the golden rule, your cue remains the desire to ensure you secure the contract. Your routine could be changed from being anxious to being comfortable, so that you can give the client space to talk and address their specific queries and concerns. The reward will still be feeling good that you've impressed your client. In fact, they are likely to be far more impressed if they feel they have been listened to, heard, and understood.

CONTEXTUAL BINDING

Learning happens by a process of association. If A and B occur together, they become associated. We can take this a step further. A and B are associated not just with one other, but also with the *context* in which they occurred. This is called 'contextual binding'. Contextual binding isn't only about your physical location, it also involves the thoughts and emotions you're experiencing at a given moment. As you read this page, changes in your thoughts are causing your mental context to change.

This contextual binding is at work when you are implementing your new leadership skills. Your brain's search process is a bit like an internet search engine. You're more likely to find what you're looking for if your search terms closely match the source content. In any given situation, your brain is rapidly rifling through your memories for ones that most closely resemble your current state of context. You may have noticed that when you're sad about something you tend to remember other sad events from your life. So contextual binding is valuable when both learning and implementing new leadership skills.

Building and retaining new leadership habits means understanding the context, focusing on specific aspects with some energy. The Neuroleadership Institute refers to this as the AGES approach for memory retention. AGES = Attention, Generation, Emotion, and Spacing.[2]

Attention

Attention engages your hippocampus, the part of the brain responsible for creating long-term memories. This means learning is most effective if you take it in bite-sized chunks. If you find yourself getting distracted, stop and take a break.

Generation

Your brain stores knowledge in a web of interconnected pieces related to one another. As you learn, you generate connections to things and experiences you already know. As you read, you will think of situations where you recall that same bit of knowledge, mark it, and attach it.

Emotion

As you have an emotional reaction to new information, allow it, enable it, and use it. Your brain is turned on by emotions and sends a signal to focus attention on the information in order to store the learning in your long-term memory.

Spacing

Space your learning, so there are reflecting times between study sessions. The longer the time you take on a particular aspect of learning, the longer the spacing time should be before studying again.

Sometimes, giving a task to yourself to embody your learning can be a powerful way of making the learning more concrete.

CASE STUDY – OVERLOADED

A client of mine, Bill, is a busy executive. He was struggling with how much responsibility he had to carry. After talking to him at length, it became apparent that this problem was mostly due to his over-commitment and perfectionism, rather than his workload. His work stress wasn't confined to the office, though. He also took his worries home with him.

I gave him some homework. After securing his absolute commitment to carry out the task I set him for two weeks, no matter what. I gave him a briefcase and told him to fill it with heavy books and carry it with him everywhere he went. He had to take it with him to client sessions, meetings, the bathroom, home, everywhere. Each time he found the briefcase to be a nuisance, he was instructed to tell himself, 'This is my perfectionism, I need it all the time.' I left it up to Bill to decide how to explain the continual presence of the briefcase to people at work and to his wife.

Two weeks later, Bill came to see me again with his briefcase in hand. He told me he had filled it with his technical books, then smiled, opened the case, and tipped the books into my waste bin. 'Burn them,' he said. 'I know that stuff, I don't need to over-prepare anymore.'

Building good leadership habits and reducing bad habits requires perseverance. We need to persist when in doubt, and enhance our self-worth.

Your capacity to be resilient and persevere has little to do with your technical skills and intellectual powers, and significantly more to do with your sense of self-worth. If we don't believe in ourselves we don't sustain our efforts to improve. We give up too easily. This aspect is addressed in the two obstacles below.

There are numerous leadership personality tests available, so we can be in MBTIed, DISCed, OCIed, TMSed, and classified as a lion, otter, golden retriever, or beaver. Deep down inside, in spite of the results, most of us don't believe we are an otter or a golden retriever, or an ISTJ Inspector, or a cautious type, and we certainly don't believe we could be classified outside the favoured green segment on the Organisational Culture Inventory (OCI) measure.

MINDSETS AND LEADERSHIP

All of these personality tests tie in with the persistent delusion that when we are at work we somehow stop being ourselves.

Breaking news! The person you are, who has been developing all your life, is the person you bring to work. You bring your own personality to work, not some flat-pack version of a personality that you assemble from a kit.

Moreover, you bring your mindset to work. These unconscious brain patterns shape what you pay attention to, what you overlook, and what you miss entirely. Each of us has a unique mindset, so we need a unique process to learn and lead effectively.

Mindsets are currently broadly defined as being either 'growth' or fixed'. However, I tend to think that mindsets are not binary or set for each individual. For example, I have a growth mindset for leadership and a fixed mindset for playing golf. Mindsets are similar to mental models, belief systems, and worldviews.

We each have a complex set of attitudes and beliefs that we use to filter perceptions in order to create meaning. Understanding and knowing what your brain actually does is the cornerstone of truly changing and getting what you want.

CHANGING YOURSELF

Getting what you want as a leader can require getting other people to change. As we all know, but often seem to overlook, most of us are resistant to being changed.

Moreover, we all tend to become more resistant the more we are pressured to change. To support a new direction, we need to believe in it in some way, especially if the new direction is quite different from our habitual direction. This means that getting what you want is rooted in convincing the other person they want the same things.

Everything we do is persuasion or influence, we are just not very aware of it. Influential leadership requires you to be conscious and deliberate about *how* you persuade others. If you deliberately try to persuade someone in an unethical direction that is poor form. If you are conscientiously persuading someone for honourable and positive reasons, that is influential communication.

Influential leadership also means changing yourself. In the same way that we are resistant to external forces that pressure us to change, we resist changing ourselves if we feel we are being compelled to do so. All our internal 'should' instructions are resisted. All changes to please a partner, teacher, boss, or parent are not real changes. *You need to really want to change.* People resist being 'made' to change. They may comply, and conform, but rarely cooperate.

Our brains are wired for familiar patterns and behaviours. It often feels easier and more comfortable to stick with what we know. Changing our behaviour and mindset requires a change in our brain pathways, and persevering in using those pathways until the new pattern or behaviour is more familiar than the old.

It's what sports people do after a missed shot. They do a practise swing, or serve, or bowl again in order to anchor the stroke they should have played into their brain pathway. It is a physical, visual representation, designed to embed the memory in the mind.

NEW LEARNINGS FORM BRAIN MAPS

Brain maps are electro-chemical representations of what exists where. They reduce a ton of intricate data into a simple, easily graspable format.

Your brain does not simply record a face or some other personal detail. Rather, it links together diverse social characteristics. This mapping also tracks social hierarchies and biological relations.

For example, the demands of a boss and a team member may be valued differently. This could be because our brains confer different statuses to the different social relationships, such as 'look up to', 'look down on' or 'the same'.

Your brain is not fixed. It can develop new pathways and new habits – if you practise. The fancy word for this is **neuroplasticity.** The brain can always find new ways of navigating our internal and external world, no matter how old we are. There is also strong evidence of the brain's ability to rebuild after some areas of the brain are damaged.

Try a little bit of neuroplasticity yourself. Notice which hand you use to clean a bench top. If you're right-handed you don't ever *decide* to use your right hand, you just grab the cloth and start cleaning. For one week, deliberately make yourself use the other hand.

At first you will find you forget to swap hands. Then, when you do use your other hand, it will feel weird and clumsy and you will want to stop. It will feel uncomfortable. If you persevere for a week it will begin to feel more natural and familiar. If you persisted for six months, it would be the new normal.

This activity shows how we can take what was a simple brain pathway action and change it. The same is true when it comes to the brain pathways that prevent you from being an influential leader.

If you don't change your brain, you cannot develop your leadership. Your brain is unique, so your leadership is unique.

CONTEMPORARY LEADERSHIP THEMES

It is easy to turn important leadership qualities into fixed mantras that may be used in unhelpful ways and not as positive leadership communication. The following examples show areas where good leadership qualities need to be applied with selective sophistication.

Authenticity

Authenticity requires being real and representing one's true nature or beliefs – being true to oneself. People trust and value genuine leaders. However, most people do not feel they can be their authentic self in the workplace.

Authentic leadership requires humility and strength. It requires admitting when you don't know something, and when you need help. It also requires acknowledging when you don't agree with something.

However, wide-open authenticity may not beneficial.

It is entirely possible to be an authentic jerk. You can authentically lose your temper or lie. Leadership authenticity needs to be coupled with self-awareness, emotional management, and an understanding of office politics.

More confusingly, a number of studies have shown that people's feelings of authenticity are often shaped by something other than being true to themselves. Feelings of authenticity seem to be related to a kind of social conformity.

Openness

Openness means providing unrestricted access to knowledge and information, as well as ensuring there is collaborative or cooperative management and decision-making. Openness can be said to be the opposite of secrecy. Leaders who are open are more trusted and more engaging. They exude a warmth that increases safety and risk-taking.

But leaders also need to be aware of privacy, confidentiality, office politics, and common sense. There are some genuine 'in confidence' matters in any organisation.

Transparency

When you're transparent, you invite trust by revealing that you have nothing to hide. You establish yourself as an honest, credible person in the eyes of others. The prospect of being open and vulnerable may make you nervous, but it is an essential feature of an effective, influential leader.

Transparency without a shield, however, can be unsafe. As a leader you need to assess the other person carefully before displaying too much transparency. You need to recognise when, where, and with whom to be transparent. With the right people it builds trust, with the wrong people it destroys trust.

Vulnerability

A vulnerable leader is unguarded with their heart, mind, and soul. Being vulnerable happens when you trust completely. Vulnerability is the surrender of personal power, in regards to letting someone close enough to harm you.

A vulnerable leader can be respected for modelling that being human is valued and effective in the workplace.

Vulnerability is the leadership quality that many people struggle with. Who wants to expose themselves to emotional damage? We feel safest when we think we are in control, watching what we say and do.

Vulnerability is the most sensitive and personally challenging skill. It requires the most sophisticated maturity, self-confidence, and street smarts to show your vulnerability.

Few businesses are completely safe and supportive. Most of us carry our insecurities carefully packed away inside somewhere, and there are those who will seize another person's vulnerability as a chance to keep one step ahead.

Vulnerability is an important leadership quality. However, it needs to be used judiciously, with carefully selected and completely trusted confidants.

Empathy

Empathy is the ability to understand and share the feelings of another. It is an awareness of, or identification with, others.

The empathic leader is able to activate connections with others. Empathy is the essence of genuine familiarity and trust. Without empathy, connection with team members is cold and constructed. Empathy is a strong skill, not a soft skill.

However, empathy requires constant reforming of self-understanding and self-awareness. Without true depth it can be superficial sympathy. Alternatively, with too much depth it can be overwhelming and hard to handle. It is not effective leadership to be more upset about your colleague's problem than they are. True empathy requires having a deep understanding of your own feelings, and a deep understanding of the other person's feelings.

Mindfulness

Mindfulness is a repackaging of the Buddhist philosophy of living in the moment.

As a leadership quality, mindfulness is the psychological process of bringing one's attention to experiences occurring in the present moment. It is also a resilience and stress-management process. Although mindfulness may be connected to meditation, it should not be confused with it. Mindfulness is a way to develop emotional maturity and competence.

Communication

An old definition about communication says that it is the act of transferring information from one place, person, or group to another. Every communication involves at least one sender, a message, and a recipient.

Communication is still vastly underestimated as a leadership skill. Talking is a quality to be mastered, yet true communication also involves numerous other aspects, such as non-verbal messages, tone of voice, location, expectation, and bias.

EFFECTIVE AND INFLUENTIAL LEADERSHIP

Three core skills of influential leaders:
- Skills are behavioural. You are not born a leader, you train hard to become one. Daily.
- Skills are paradoxical. Sometimes the most effective leadership behaviour is to do something unexpected and unusual.
- Skills are interrelated. One or two skills are not enough – you need a complete toolkit.[3]

Effective, influential leadership is about adaptability. This means developing the capacity to see things from different perspectives – nearly all the time. Leadership is built on our personal values and principles. But when you are faced with a stressful situation at work, do you take the time to consider how your values and principles relate to the matter? As an effective leader, you need to check your inner compass.

Values are subjective, internal, and can change over time. Values represent the moral, social, and political aspects of those things we consider important. A healthy workplace invests in all three types.

Values can be things like respect, honesty, fairness, and compassion. They are often plastered over offices like wallpaper. However, my experience is that they can feel meaningless for many staff, if they don't see those values enacted.

While value statements are questionable for whole organisations, they are essential things to have in your carry-on case as an influential leader. It guides how you will behave and what you will be like with others.

Principles are fundamental truths that are permanent, unchanging, and universal in nature. We use them as our moral compass. They guide the decisions we make about our lives, and drive our values and goals. There needs to be guiding principles against which you hold every decision and action you take. A good one for influential leadership is some variation on, 'Always do what's right.'

MOTIVATION

You need to be motivated to change yourself into being a more influential leader. There are two main types of motivation – push and pull.

Push motivation is a behaviour that we are forced to complete, by ourselves or others, in order to satisfy a need or to achieve a goal. Push motivation is external.

Pull motivation is a behaviour that we feel drawn to – it is internal.

Push motivation is rough. It's exhausting, depleting, and requires constant willpower, which quickly burns out. Push motivation acts in response to others. Forcing things to happen complicates and ultimately breaks them.

Pull motivation is much more powerful. It draws you forward and actually gives you more energy while you're doing it. Wanting to do something makes the experience easy and pleasurable

Pull motivation is powered by a chirpy little chemical called dopamine, which creates positive emotions like satisfaction and enjoyment. Naturally, you want your teams to be driven by positive emotions. But this may not be easy to achieve, because the effects of rewarding people often don't last.

The reason for this is that neurons quickly experience habituation, where nothing is ever as good as the first time. The response to any reward diminishes with each repetition, so that we quickly become bored and want the next new thing. Something that starts as an unexpected pleasure quickly becomes something we feel entitled to, before beginning to seem as though it isn't enough.

As a leader, knowing this about habituation helps you stop feeling frustrated when your carefully crafted rewards and incentives produce few results.

By varying the incentives and finding new ways of recognising and encouraging good effort, you can help keep your teams operating on pull motivation.

Your brain uses a system of neurons, which exchange information using chemical and electric signals called 'action potentials'. These action potentials form pathways created by our learned experience.

Neurons allow you to make sense of every action, thought, and feeling you will ever have. This is the biological basis of learning. The more you practise a certain behaviour, such as mindfulness or anxiety, the more ingrained the relevant neuronal pathways become.

Your brain is malleable, like Play-Doh, and your repeated experiences determine its shape. Over time, and with enough repetition, the neuronal pathways in your brain can change, which is neuroplasticity in action.

Neurons favour novel information, and so unusual events will catch your attention more than those that you are familiar with. Consider this in terms of leadership at work.

There are areas of the brain that play a central role when it comes to leadership:

• The amygdala.
• The prefrontal cortex.

The amygdala, unchecked by the prefrontal cortex, is sort of the bad guy. It is our ancient protective reaction to danger. It is responsible for the perception of emotions such as anger, fear, and sadness, as well as the controlling of aggression.

Having these feelings is good. Moderating them is essential for wellbeing. The amygdala helps to store memories of events and emotions so that you can recognise similar events in the future. Researchers also refer to the amygdala as the primitive brain or lizard brain.

The prefrontal cortex is the good guy, and controls important cognitive skills such as emotional expression, problem-solving, memory, language, judgment, and sexual behaviours. It is the social control panel for your personality and your communication.

The amygdala is basically a neurological mouse trap. Usually, the trap is very finely tuned, so that any slight intrusion to get to the cheese sets off the trap instantly and it snaps. This is the fight or flight response. The panic buying of toilet rolls during COVID-19 is a demonstration of how our amygdala still reacts today.

The amygdala supports a variety of functions, such as memory formation, and governs emotions such as fear, anxiety, and anger.

In times of stress, you experience a fight or flight reaction, unless your amygdala is moderated by the prefrontal cortex.

WHAT IS REAL?

There are two brain features that limit leadership development. These two aspects are the hidden ways in which you handle your work relationships at every single moment.

1. The constant impact of your amygdala on many of our daily encounters.
2. The way your brain selects small bits of all the data around us and inside us. The amygdala is fine tuned for utility, not reality.

The first of these two features triggers your fight or flight response, so that you quickly react with anger or fear, even though the situation may not require such reactions.

The second pushes you to unquestioningly accept too many generalisations, and from this you develop your biases and prejudices.

When it comes to changing these responses, the difficulty is that you are so conditioned to believe that what you experience is reality. In fact, you only pay attention to a small part of what you experience and then generalise and construct the data from those small pieces of information.

So you have to ask yourself — is the world you see around you the real world, or an internal perceptual copy of that world generated by neural processes in your brain? Your thinking, beliefs, desires, and motivations can exert significant influence on basic perceptual processes.

What you see, hear, and smell is shaped by what you think. The way you normally think about your feelings and emotions simply doesn't measure up with what neuroscience reveals about what your brain actually does and what's really going on.

You might accept that even space and time are not necessarily elements of external reality. For example, consider the common experience of time slowing down when you are bored or speeding up when you are in love. And the daydream of being somewhere else that seems so real until you get yelled at for weaving out of your lane. Within this conception, only a certain part of reality, which you need for mastering life, is projected onto space and time.

Your mind is not merely an observer, which perceives reality as it is. Your mind actually changes and shapes your reality. This obviously impacts on your leadership behaviour. Your biases are a prison you are not even aware of. They are your default settings. It is sobering to remember this when you are telling someone you are right, and they are wrong.

ACCOUNTABILITY IS IN YOUR HEAD

The neuroscientists say that about five times a second, at an unconscious level, your brain is taking in all the data in the environment around us and the amygdala is assessing whether it is safe or dangerous.

If your amygdala is unsure about a situation, it will immediately default to rating that situation as unsafe, and prepare for fight or flight.

Your brain takes in every tiny bit of information, and codes and stores it in various parts of your brain. Then, when you need that information again, you are able to reconstruct it. The way your brain works helps you consider more carefully the two key aspects of influential leadership: accountability and responsibility.

EXAMPLE – NON-EMPATHIC LEADERSHIP

When I bristle and react to something that someone says to me I actually am *choosing* to bristle. The other person didn't make me bristle. Even though it feels like they did. It all happens incredibly quickly, but within milliseconds, I select 'bristling' as a response out of the multitude of possible reactions to what they said. Here's a millisecond-by-millisecond breakdown of what's happening inside my brain.

At the planning meeting, Carol says to me, *'No Graham, you've got that completely wrong.'* She uses a stern voice, has a frown on her face, and avoids eye contact with me. The auditory message and visual signals are coded into electrical impulses which zap along a brain pathway.

The message bangs into the amygdala guard, who says, '*She's obviously attacking you. There's no real threat in office politics, so there's no need to run. Strike back!*'

My prefrontal cortex chimes in and says, '*Hey wait a minute, you're in the middle of a meeting, it's not really a big deal, discuss it with her later.*'

Amygdala: '*No. Screw it. Get her now, otherwise it will get worse before the next promotion round.*'

Prefrontal cortex: '*You're making too much of this, you're in a much better position than she is, and anyway, it's not a big deal.*'

Amygdala: '*No, get her now.*'

I then bristle and react to Carol with a biting retort.

My choice.

This doesn't mean I shouldn't get bristly and react. I can. However, I also need to accept responsibility for my reaction. If Carol complains about my behaviour then it's on me, not her. If my boss chews me out for the way I reacted, I am accountable.

This scenario is a snapshot of non-empathic leadership in action.

An empathic leadership example would have me stopping at the first prefrontal interjection, letting it go, and chatting with her later to share my perception.

So What Are The Barriers To Empathic Leadership?

As a species, even though we do not face many of the same dangers as our ancient ancestors, we still perceive insults, strangers, and unusual environments as potential threats. This means that your first primitive reaction is one of fear and protection. This is so automatic and so outside your awareness that you hardly even notice it. You just react. Sometimes without even feeling the emotion.

To fully assess every threat and every issue is far too time-consuming, chaotic, and unmanageable. Therefore, you develop brain pathways that form generalisations about what is very safe, what is quite safe, what is unsafe, what is dangerous, and what is life-threatening. You then bunch the data into the appropriate categories.

Mostly, these generalisations and brain pathways are helpful and serve you well. Oftentimes, however, they become fixed because your prejudices and biases aren't necessarily accurate or helpful. For instance, some unhelpful beliefs would be that flying in aeroplanes is dangerous, all spiders are deadly, people with a different skin colour can't be trusted, old people are stupid, money is great, and so on.

Simplistically, if you perceive a threat then you react from your amygdala. If you are keen to be an empathic leader then you moderate your primal reaction with your prefrontal cortex, based upon a more sophisticated assessment of the person or situation. How quickly you reassess things, and understand that you are actually safe, is a measure of your emotional intelligence and maturity.

Your biases and prejudices will sit there forever unless you actively do something about them. However, your amygdala ensures you have several very embedded and persistent ways of responding to the world. Outside of your consciousness it is behind every action you take and every thought you have.

This means that you can't just rely on your prefrontal cortex to rescue you. There are times when a really potent and very unexpected threat will occur at work, and you need to be ready way before it hits you. This means you need to understand a few things about why you feel threatened and uncomfortable.

CALMING THE AMYGDALA

Here are the four key ways you can spot when your amygdala is taking over your leadership:

Simplicity – you like things that you can process quickly, without having to struggle to understand what is happening. This isn't an intelligence issue. Everyone gets stressed when things become too complicated. When it comes to leadership, we do not like complex tasks or demanding people.

Beware of a desire to over-simplify matters.

Speed – you want a quick reaction time, especially with stressful and uncomfortable situations. The amygdala wants a quick-fix. In the context of leadership, this means you prefer short-term solutions to long-term strategies.

Assess whether the matter needs a quick reaction or a more strategic approach.

Safety – people do everything to maintain safety and avoid threat. Any perceived threat is bad, so the default position is to avoid difficult conversations. You protect yourself first and foremost. In a leadership situation, this means your decision-making prioritises safety over solutions.

This is risk-averse leadership. Learn how to have difficult conversations, and take significant but safe risks.

Size – people manage small numbers better than large. We don't like groups bigger than eight, and we don't like calculus. In terms of leadership, one-on-one issues can be hard, managing teams is a real worry, and culture change of the whole organisation is overwhelming.

This means having a relatively small number of team members to supervise, planning big culture changes in stages, and taking longer than you might expect.

There are many perceptual tricks your brain learns to perform so you can navigate your world.

For instance, your brain only 'sees' a two-dimensional world. Distant objects appear on the same plane as close objects. This means that you perceive a bus 20 metres away and a person standing in front as a small bus and a big person. Your brain learns to translate distance, so you interpret what you are seeing as a person in the foreground, and a bus in the background. In reality, though, your brain still sees in two dimensions.

Motion perception is similar. You may have been sitting in your car at the traffic lights, and glanced at the car in the next lane. You see and feel as though you are moving backwards, and so you hit the brakes. Then you discover that in reality you aren't moving at all! The car next to you is moving forward.

In the same way, it is possible to address some of your own perceptions and limiting behaviours your changes will result in better leadership behaviours.

MAKING A MOTIVATED COMMITMENT TO CHANGE

Much of our natural inclination is to control or change other people. If you have raised toddlers and teenagers you have all the proof you need that you can't make people do things they don't want to do.

What you can do, though, is to change yourself. Coming to terms with this reality is crucial to leadership.

As psychologists, it is our belief that an influential leader needs to have the capacity to create a work environment in such way that each person is uniquely motivated to achieve the organisational goals, and feels recognised for so doing.

The leader is responsible for creating and maintaining the work culture. An influential leader builds a living, flexible culture.

People want to be listened to, and they want to be understood. You can't fake this by pretending to listen and understand. You have to genuinely listen and actually understand. If you do not listen and understand, then it is not possible to be truly influential.

There are two major obstacles that you need to overcome in order to be able to create this motivating and flexible culture. All of us face these two challenges whenever we seriously think about ourselves and our relationships with our fellow humans at work.

OBSTACLE ONE – THE FEAR OF FEELING UNCOMFORTABLE

You are reading this book for a reason. There is something about your leadership that you want to change. Change is rarely comfortable, which is why it requires commitment. You need to overcome your natural inertia.

Think about why you bought the book, and what you hope to gain from reading it. When you are clear about what you want to gain, make it into a commitment.

This is your personal promise to yourself. It is your contract to put real effort into changing, in ways that will be habitual and sustained. Your promise to yourself will be created using your self-knowledge about the ways you often sabotage commitments.

It might look something like this:

'I commit to working on my influential leadership for half an hour every day.'

'I commit to persevering with my leadership development for nine months.'

'I will tell two significant people about my leadership commitment.'

'I will practise one new aspect of influential leadership every month.'

Write this commitment down as a sentence.

EXERCISE – COMMITMENT SENTENCE

'I am committed to

....

....

Reflect on this commitment sentence for a while. Then put it somewhere safe because you will be returning to it quite often.

So far, making this commitment has been a pretty low-risk exercise.

What if you told your partner or a friend about your commitment? How would that feel?

What if you told your team members? Or your boss?

The thought of sharing this information may trigger a variety of emotions.

Research shows that naming our emotions is a big step towards managing them. So what precisely are you feeling about your commitment? Are you scared, unsure, anxious, panicky, or stressed?

Where does this feeling reside? Is it in your stomach, throat, head, hands, or legs?

Understanding what you are feeling will help you to maintain your commitment.

Once you have created your commitment sentence, you need to make a plan of when, where, and how you will take action. This means you can now expand your sentence into a statement.

Your commitment statement will have several parts to it.

1.	What personal changes am I going to make?
2.	When will I make them?
3.	Which aspects of my leadership am I going to start applying these changes to?

4. Who is the safest person to start my change with?

5. How will I know that I am starting to be successful?

EXERCISE – COMMITMENT STATEMENT

1. The personal changes I am going to make are

....
....
....
....

2. The time frame I will make these changes in is

....
....
....
....

3. I will start by applying these changes to the following aspects of my leadership

....
....
....
....

4. The safest person to start my change with is

....
....
....
....

5. I will know that I am starting to be successful when

....

....

....

....

It is important to remember that all effective change is a work in progress. This means you need to be open to making mistakes.

The thought of making mistakes can feel uncomfortable.

We learn to fear uncomfortable feelings, but if we stay with what we know, we don't expand our leadership potential. By using 'propelling questions' we can activate new neural pathways and open up new possibilities.

Propelling questions are those that combine an audacious goal with a significant constraint. Not questions like, 'How can I be a great leader' or 'How can I increase my leadership skills?' But questions, such as, 'How can I take some real risks as a leader?'

Your commitment statement requires that you take action, not that you *try* to take action.

OBSTACLE TWO – THE FEAR OF NOT BEING IN CONTROL

Risk may mean a loss of control, the danger of exposure, the possibility of getting things wrong, and, ultimately, failure.

Fear of risk is your amygdala's default position. People often try to control things they can't control, and don't try to control things they can control. Our obsession with ownership is a big part of trying to be in control. The need for ownership is a significant leadership limitation.

'That's my desk, my project, my idea, my decision.' We all assume we own things, but we don't really own anything. We make the idea of control so important.

As part of relinquishing control, 'That's mine' needs to be replaced with, 'I hold that in trust for others'. This means that you are both accountable for yourself, and acting in the service of others.

You can only control your own actions. To make a true difference as a leader, you need to enable your teams by ensuring they can be responsible for *their* own actions. Therefore, attempting to take control of everything is not a successful leadership method.

So, fear of risk is a big obstacle, because letting go of control is a big risk, even as a step towards influential leadership.

Leaders with seniority try not to expose themselves to making mistakes. This is exhausting, and also ignores the reality that doing nothing is itself unhelpful.

When you make mistakes you expose yourself to learning and increasing your knowledge. Being safe keeps you from acquiring wisdom. We are taught that failure is bad, and yet everything we achieve in life is built on learning through failure. We learn to walk, talk, and ride a bicycle by failing hundreds of times. The value of making mistakes and being vulnerable are cleverly detailed by Kathryn Schulz, in *Being Wrong: Adventures in the Margin of Error,* and by Brené Brown in *Dare to Lead.*[4]

GETTING THINGS WRONG

We all get things wrong. But it is often easier for us to take the view that we are right and others are wrong. We confuse 'belief' with 'truth'.

Our beliefs are so enmeshed with who we are that being wrong can easily wound our sense of self. This means that when we think we know something, we have the conviction of rightness whether we're right or not. For these reasons very few people are comfortable saying, '*I was wrong*' or '*I don't know*'.

So the ability to recognise that we are not infallible, and that an error may be ours or, at least, partly ours, is a sign of greater empathy and imagination. Recognising that we can be wrong requires courage, but it is essential for growth and leadership.

The fact that we tend to be blind to our own errors is exactly the reason that we need to increase our self-awareness, encourage feedback, and receive other external information about our behaviours. The thought of this kind of input can feel threatening because it is likely to require us to challenge our beliefs. And challenging our beliefs can leave us feeling vulnerable.

We almost always view our own vulnerabilities more negatively than we view other people's. This is probably because our thoughts about our own vulnerabilities are very concrete, whereas when we think about others' vulnerabilities we do so more abstractly. This means that even when showing vulnerability feels more like weakness from the inside, the evidence is that to others, these acts look more like courage.

Therefore, abstract assessment is associated with a more positive, risk-friendly perspective. Which means that, in spite of the way it may make us feel, expressing vulnerability is a good thing. Self-disclosure can build trust, seeking help can boost learning, and admitting mistakes can foster acceptance and forgiveness.

There is an ancient Japanese ritual, Kintsugi, which is a method for repairing broken ceramics with a special lacquer mixed with gold, silver, or platinum. The philosophy behind the technique is to recognise the value of the object and to visibly incorporate the repair into the new piece instead of hiding the mistake by disguising it.

Interestingly, this approach recognises the beauty in the mess of vulnerable situations. At an individual and organisational level, this means ensuring a psychologically safe context. This is 'street smarts' vulnerability.

Almost everyone shares one insecurity—the fear of not being good enough. We compensate for this fear by being perfectionistic, controlling, avoiding, or faking it. We don't believe others share our fear, but they do. So take a small risk. Let go of some control.

When you study your life dispassionately, you will observe you are really only able to control a very, very tiny bit of it. Shit happens outside our control all the time, and often we feel bad about that. Particularly if we think we made a mistake that caused the shit. However, we do have the capacity to feel and react in the way we choose, and not to splash about in self-blame.

So fear of risk restricts our personhood and our leadership. Being less in control, allowing ourselves to be vulnerable, accepting that we may be wrong, and even that we may even fail, are all necessary steps to becoming an effective leader.

So, what do you need to do to prepare to take this risk?

You may remember the first time you jumped off a diving board, or rode a bike, or spoke in public – the feeling in the pit of your stomach, the excitement, the drama, and the false starts. But you really wanted to do it. And then you did! The experience then shifts to relief, joy, and surprise, when you discover it wasn't that scary after all.

What do you believe you are risking by making personal changes?

Is the risk that you will appear to be weak? Or that you may hurt other people's feelings if you become more honest and direct? Do you believe that delegating responsibility will damage your business? Or that people won't like the 'real you'?

EXERCISE – PERCEIVED RISKS

Write down what you believe will be the biggest risk for you in becoming a more influential leader.

The biggest risk I am taking is

....
....
....
....

Now you recognise what it is that you fear most, think about what you can do to make the risk worthwhile.

To make the risk worthwhile, I can

....
....
....
....

You have got through the two obstacles of making the commitment and taking a risk. Which means you can begin to take action.

2

HOW TO START BEING AN INFLUENTIAL LEADER

'Emotions are the key to communication and understanding. They are parts, highly complex and messy parts, of reasoning itself.'
— **Martha Nussbaum**

SIX PROPOSITIONS OF LEADERSHIP

How do the following statements fit in with your understanding of leadership?

1. You are the only person who needs to change.
2. You need to take time and prepare comprehensively.
3. You need to manage and reduce your own biases and ego.
4. You need to use the same speech, body language, and outlook as your counterpart.

5.   You will build connection and trust by mirroring the nature of your counterpart.

6.   By following the first five steps, over time, you will achieve a shared brain connection – empathy – which will influence your counterpart.

These steps to leadership are grounded in the way our brains work. When we converse with another person, what happens at a micro level is remarkable and a little magical.

EMPATHY IS AT THE HEART OF LEADERSHIP

Empathy is the capacity to:
*   be affected by and share the emotional state of another,
*   assess the reasons for the other's state, and
*   identify with the other, adopting his or her perspective.

So empathy is taking someone at face value. The twist is that your perception of their face value comes from your personality, upbringing, and unconscious biases. This is why self-awareness is essential to see their face value objectively, and not just see what you expect to see. You need to remove your preconceptions before you can see clearly.

Most research papers about empathy include the 'feeling into' definition, which covers important leadership traits such as rapport, imitation and mimicry, pervasive empathy, automatic empathy, and facilitative empathy. As leaders we do no harm displaying these aspects of empathy.

The power of deep empathy, more than technical or professional skills, is the make or break of trust and influence. This is because non-empathic responses are judgemental and cause a disconnect in the conversation, while empathic responses are focused on the other person and are connecting in nature.

Recent research establishes that the vast majority of people consider empathy is important at work, but a large number don't experience it.

EXAMPLE – EMPATHIC AND NON-EMPATHIC RESPONSES

In this scenario, a colleague announces they have just been told off by the boss.

Non-empathic responses include:

'Tell someone who cares.'

'Yeah, she told me off last week. She had a problem with my presentation.'

'What did you do wrong?'

'You need to get used to it. She isn't really mean.'

Empathic responses include:

'Oh, sorry that happened. What did she say?'

'That must be upsetting. How are you feeling?'

'Would you like to talk about it?'

'Yuk. How did it end up?'

In this scenario, a colleague announces they have a great idea for a new project.

Non-empathic responses include:

'I had an idea for a project too. It involves doing...'

'That would never work around here.'

'I think that has already been tried before.'

Empathic responses include:

'Wow. How did you come up with that?'

'Tell me about it in more detail.'

'You are certainly making a real contribution.'

It is also important to consider the body language that goes with these two different responses. With non-empathic responses there will be non-verbal cues such as frowns, grimaces, an irritated voice tone, and looking away. With empathic responses there will be non-verbal cues such as; smiles, a pleasant tone of voice, thumbs up or high-fives, and facing towards the other person.

EXAMPLE – EMPATHY AND EMAILS

Consider the non-verbal message in this email:

TO: Laura
CC: Laura's Boss.
Subject: Our conversation yesterday
Laura, you were clearly very confused about what was being asked of you. You need to resolve this immediately.

Why CC the boss? Why not discuss the issue face-to-face? This non-empathic email will lead to an escalation of the problem.

If you need to say something personal, say it personally.

If the person is just down the corridor, don't email – walk down and speak with them.

Don't copy other people in on a private matter.

EMPATHY IS A VERY HARD SKILL

With positive face-to-face connections between people, you build empathy and trust. Empathy enables you to identify other people's feelings, prevents you from making rapid decisions, and helps you create wiser solutions.

With empathic leadership the *relationship* is front of mind. Research indicates that companies with a culture of productive and contented employees have empathy at their core. Empathy develops when trusted individuals interact. These interactions create cognitive coupling between these individuals' brains.

Cognitive coupling is no soft skill. It requires practise to have a high level of awareness of both your own emotions, and other peoples'. The more experienced you are with this awareness, the better you will develop your capacity to communicate and lead effectively.

BARRIERS TO EMPATHY – TRUTH AND PERCEPTION

How often have you seen a movie, eaten a meal, or met someone, and in discussing your judgement of the movie, meal, or person with a friend, discovered that you have opposing viewpoints?

This is an example of reality versus perception, but the focus here is more on your *reaction.* When you discover that you have an opposing viewpoint to someone, the reaction is often to believe that you are right and they are wrong.

This belief is a barrier to empathy. When you 'click' with someone else, you are not just simply sharing another's feelings or emotions. The other person is experienced as another being *like you* through an appreciation of similarity. You are in the same tribe or group.

When everyone lived as tribes, they shared the same experiences, enjoyed the same food, and fought and fled together. They had the same worldview. However, as your worldview becomes more complex, empathy becomes an effort, and those feelings of familiarity and similarity are weakened. You become right and others become wrong.

Empathic communication overrides this sense of 'right' and 'wrong'. It enables actions, emotions, and sensations experienced by others to become meaningful to you, because they become shared experiences. This strengthens feelings of similarity and familiarity. This is important for leadership, because those feelings of similarity and familiarity enable you to have influence.

INTERPERSONAL CONNECTION

The way your brain creates the before, during, and after experience of being an influential leader is surprising. Your brain has two functional aspects – the conscious 'thinking' mind, and the unconscious 'doing' mind. The conscious mind determines actions, the unconscious mind determines reactions.

Your conscious mind is linear, sequential, and logical. It likes everything to make sense. It has limited capabilities, compared to the unconscious mind. Your conscious mind is the part of your brain that you are using to read and process these words.

Your unconscious mind takes the words and creates meaning from them, especially how the meaning relates to you. The unconscious mind is a reservoir of feelings, thoughts, urges, and memories that are outside of our conscious awareness.

The empirical evidence suggests that the unconscious mind is responsible for our repressed feelings, automatic skills, automatic reactions, biases, phobias, and desires.

Nearly all of your brain's work is conducted at the unconscious level, completely without your knowledge. So everything you do is programmed by your unconscious mind, outside of your awareness.

The amygdala can be informed about something threatening before the cortex has a clue. Further, the amygdala is super-sensitive, so that it responds to stimuli that are too fleeting or too faint for the cortex to even notice.

At work, this means you can be happily running an executive meeting when your amygdala catches the faintest smirk from Mark, the finance director. Your throat constricts a tiny bit, you hesitate for a second, and then seemingly out of nowhere you snap at him.

In milliseconds, your brain assesses a massive amount of information about another human face. You are constantly reading non-verbal cues when you interact face-to-face, and you get better and better at it through close observation and matching. With this contact, specialised brain cells are triggered. And if you deem the connection to be trustworthy, your system secretes oxytocin, dopamine, serotonin, and vasopressin.

Dopamine gives you a feeling of excitement and a surge of energy when you find things that meet your needs; oxytocin produces the feeling of being safe and helps you to connect with and trust others. When present, oxytocin fuels our sense of belonging and attachment to groups; serotonin produces the feeling of being respected by others and a sense of pride.

Conversely, if there is a negative connection, you subliminally feel fear or anger. Your amygdala gets in on the act and releases epinephrine (adrenaline) and norepinephrine (noradrenaline) into the bloodstream, along with a dash of cortisol.

This causes an increase in heart rate, muscle strength, blood pressure, and sugar metabolism. So the brain uses the negative emotion to gear up the body to fight or to run.

Mostly you make the assessment of trustworthiness unconsciously. Not only do you *connect* with a well-matched person, but neuroscience has established *you rewire your own brain and the other person's.*

This is called mirroring, interpersonal neural synchronisation (INS), or neural coupling. Active matching means you communicate so effectively you share meaning, delight, fear, and hope – and brain chemicals.

A negative encounter also changes you, but not for the better. It is the office rivals, bitter or competitive. It is the offended client who sues you. In groups it is the dysfunctional team, or the toxic culture of a badly led organisation.

So how do you harness the power of empathy?

One of the most powerful human interactions you can have is face-to-face contact involving eye gaze. Eyes are powerful. If you put up a large picture of a pair of eyes at a bus stop, people become more likely to clean up litter. Post a picture of eyes in a workplace coffee room, and the money paid on the honour system triples. Show a pair of eyes on a computer screen and people become more generous in online computer games.

From the first instance of eye contact, specialised brain cells are activated. If the gaze is warm or even neutral, our brain experiences a positive release of chemicals.

The neuropeptide oxytocin is crucial to feeling safe, and encourages affiliation and trusting behaviour. Direct, supportive eye gaze activates oxytocin, and such positive engagement activates empathic pathways. The more you look up and engage, the more you read both the affect and effect you have on people, the stronger our connection becomes.

Even positive eye contact between an anxious person and someone they trust assists in synchronisation of various brain regions, quietening the sympathetic nervous system and amygdala, and reducing the person's agitation.

So good leadership needs eye contact. Eye contact helps you connect, which in turn helps neural coupling, rewiring your brain and those of the people you interact with. It is worth noting that in some cultures, direct eye contact is not accepted. In this instance, look at the person's cheekbone instead.

This capacity for neural connecting gets a synchronised routine going, deepening your perception of the other person, and switching you into discernment mode. It alters your perspective from reactive to receptive problem-solving. This, in turn, minimises short-term decisions and forms different neural pathways, which nurture foresight and wisdom.

This means that in a leadership encounter you will not be so quick to dismiss that curve-ball idea. You are likely to evaluate its worth with more open-mindedness.

Studies have been carried out on the brains of those who had either positive or negative leaders at work, as they recalled the experience while wired up in the lab. The brains of those with positive leaders activated mirror neurons related to social and affective networks, while those with negative leaders showed a pattern of quite different mirror neurons related to avoidance, narrowed attention, decreased compassion. Leadership has a lasting impact. My favourite researcher, Dr Fiona Kerr, has found the choice is not whether the interactions we have will cause a connection. The choice is whether that connection will be positive or negative.[5]

She says neural connecting is a live, two-way engagement. The use of EEG or fNIRS to scan people when they are engaging someone through sharing a story or idea shows this recursive interaction at the neuronal level.

One consistent finding is that while people interact, the readings show a physical change in both brains. For this reason, it is always worth taking time to work with your counterpart, rather than just having a quick chat.

The evidence is that as two brains become more attuned to each other over many interactions, they get to be so synchronised with each other that we can anticipate what the other person is going to say.

Some researchers have speculated that emotional expressivity can be a more reliable signal of cooperativeness than simply feeling positive emotions. This means that investing in expressing your emotions builds better emotional coupling.

For introverts, who may feel uncomfortable with strong displays of emotional expression, this will require some practise. Consider taking drama lessons or using props such as emojis or cards. Even if being emotionally expressive doesn't feel like 'you' at first, everyone can develop new brain pathways.

In early childhood you learned to separate out all the items in your environment, such as food, parents, toys, car, neighbours, cat, dog, and so on. Everything in your environment has, at some point, been given an identity and a meaning in the field of your experience. This whole process is the same and yet entirely different for every single one of us. There are no identical realities for any of us, just shared glimpses.

However, in spite of these identities and meaning that we have all laid down, the nervous system always functions in the present. This means that in the moment of conversation you can match and lead and reframe, in order to help mould new views and alternatives. This is the mindfulness of leadership. Each moment, every moment, is an opportunity to be influential.

Neural mirroring makes person-to-person connection much more effective. By listening and observing well, you can sense what's on someone's mind and demonstrate that you care enough to understand. It's a strong need for all of us – to be understood as a person with thoughts, emotions, and intentions that are unique, and valuable, and deserving of attention.

When you mirror the actions and behaviour of others or match them, your neurons fire up the same way when you watch someone do something as when you do it yourself. That's how matching lets you *feel* the actions you see.

If you're sceptical about the influence of this tiny group of neurons think about the magic of a Grand Final or World Cup. Each foul, great mark, goal, intercept, and flow of play on the field fires up the mirror neurons that make you and the thousands of other fans share the same feelings. You become emotionally involved in something that you aren't physically doing. The intensity, the physical exhaustion, and the thrill of each player on the field are all so vivid, even if we're sitting in a sports bar hundreds of miles away from the stadium. Emotional access is the foundation of solidarity.

Empathy enables meaningful interpersonal bonds. The expression of emotions is a system of social communication. Facial and bodily movements, along with tone of voice, language use, and many other verbal and non-verbal cues, reveal preferences about our thinking and actions. This enables direct understanding in a complex exchange. Empathy is the way to simplify and agree our shared reality.

This means that coming to terms with your negative and positive emotions, and the negative and positive emotions of others, is essential for effective leadership.

PREDICTIVE LEADERSHIP

The brain's most important job is keeping your body alive. To accomplish this, it devotes most of its time to predicting what will happen next, so your body can be ready for any contingency. Tons of predictions are generated from past experience, and the ones that win are those that fit the situation in the next moment.

However, there are still times when we make prediction errors. We might misjudge the distance we need to jump over a puddle, for example, and end up with wet feet.

Some of the most important predictions your brain makes are about people. Studies show that when you meet strangers, you like and trust them more when their facial movements, such as smiling, match your brain's expectations.

You are able to understand others by their facial expressions, body gestures, and demeanour. People dislike things that are unfamiliar, and do not categorise them as suitable to engage with, but if they trigger positive emotions, they will interact with them. So if you experience a stranger as familiar, similar, and safe, then you are more likely to interact positively with them.

When you interact, you synchronise the social and emotional networks in your brain. For example, neuroscientists have found that during a musical performance, the brain activity of the audience synchronises with the brain activity of the musicians.

Synchronisation also helps you to read other people's intentions accurately. Do you remember a time where you had a blow up with someone over text or email, then cleared it up very quickly once you had spoken to them face-to-face?

One study wired-up the brains of a group of people, to investigate how leaders are chosen. The results showed that neural coupling was significantly higher between the chosen leader and the other members of the group than it was between the group members who were 'followers'. This suggests that leaders emerge by synchronising their brain effectively with the brains of their followers.

When people engage actively and positively with another person by making eye contact, leaning in closer, matching non-verbal cues, and telling stories and jokes, many studies show the brains of both people light up in the same regions. Furthermore, brain scans show there is a high level of reciprocal electrochemical activity when we help others. This is why it often feels good to do good.

Finally, the better you know someone, the quicker and more strongly you are able to synchronise. It almost feels like mind reading. Oxytocin is thought to enhance positive social 'mind-reading' encounters, and eye gaze is what gets oxytocin going.

EMPATHY AND LONGER-TERM THINKING

Empathic leadership helps you to tackle complex problems and to think strategically by shifting your focus to longer-term solutions. Empathy lengthens and deepens your view, changing the problem-solving path your brain takes. Empathy is as much about thinking and decision-making as about tuning in to others.

Linear problems usually require the application of known fixes, so your brain races back to the problem-solving approach that worked last time.

Complex problems, however, are new and unpredictable, so you need novel solutions. This means your leadership brain needs to override the old connections, take in new information, and put it together in creative ways. This requires plasticity, which means your brain needs to loosen up. It happens when your brain is flooded with empathy. Empathy and emotional engagement create strategic, longer-term thinking, new ideas, and greater flexibility.

It may seem simpler just to tell people what to do, but it doesn't work very well. When it comes to influential leadership, although it takes some effort to learn to read non-verbal cues and respond to others' emotions, once you have mastered these skills, you will be significantly more effective as a leader.

COMMUNICATION RESEARCH

Cognitive empathy is the ability to understand how a person feels and what they might be thinking. Cognitive empathy makes us better communicators because it helps us relay information in a way that best reaches the other person.

Emotional empathy, also known as affective empathy, is the ability to share the feelings of another person. Some have described it as 'your pain in my heart'. This type of empathy helps you build emotional connections with others.

Compassionate empathy, also known as empathic concern, goes beyond simply understanding other people and sharing their feelings – it actually moves us to take action, and to help however we can. The evolutionary evidence is that compassion for our tribe helped us collaborate and survive.

EXAMPLE – COGNITIVE, EMOTIONAL, AND COMPASSIONATE EMPATHY

A close friend has recently lost their job. Your natural reaction may be sympathy, a feeling of pity, or sorrow.

Empathy takes more time and effort.

Beginning with cognitive empathy, imagine what the person is going through. Why did they lose their job? How significant was their job to their career? How will their life now change?

Moving on to emotional empathy, you look for ways not only to understand your friend's feelings, but to share them. You try to connect with something in yourself that has experienced the feeling of loss and career change. You might remember how it felt when you lost a job. Emotional empathy does not mean telling the other person that you know what they are going through, it simply means looking into yourself to understand their feelings.

Finally, compassionate empathy moves you to take action. You might offer to help discuss their options, provide a resource for alternative jobs, or just allow them to vent.

If emotional empathy doesn't come naturally to you, one way of understanding what other people are feeling is to provide a scale, or rating, that you can use to gauge their level of their emotions. It can help to prevent people from feeling challenged, allowing more discussion, maintaining the relationship, and giving you the opportunity to be more persuasive if the other person scores things differently to you.

EXAMPLE – MEETING OF MINDS

Imagine that you are coming out of a meeting, and another team member doesn't seem happy.

Using a rating system, you could say that you thought the meeting was really good, and that you'd rate it nine out of ten for productivity.

By inviting the other team member to provide *their* rating, you will then be able to gauge their feelings and to explore the reasons why they feel this way.

This strategy is likely to be more effective than simply asking them if they thought the meeting was productive.

Everyone is different. If you are coming under fire and you ask the other person to give you a number out of ten to describe how upset they are, it may make things worse. You get the best out of people if you use their language. Instead, you could ask them how big the problem is or what their main areas of concern are. Essentially, you want to calibrate the other person's feelings.

This calibration approach ends the 'I'm right/you're wrong' cul-de-sac. No one is trapped into fighting or defending. It stops things being black and white. Most significantly, it is a respectful way of problem-solving. At an unconscious level, it reveals that all of our decisions are actually beliefs, not hard facts.

Our certainty about most things is only based on incomplete knowledge and limited data. By rating things on a scale we expose the probabilistic nature of our beliefs. Being flexible with your certainty is your best bet.

Your interpretation of another person's mood, behaviour, or thinking, will be shaped by your prior experience and unconscious bias. Your instincts may be wrong. So check reactions and reassess.

After you engage with others, take time to consider any feedback they provide, and amend your response accordingly.

EXERCISE – COMMUNICATION RESEARCH

We can connect this communication research with our everyday conversations. Reflect on your last few important conversations and run through them carefully in your mind. Score them against this scale:

1 = very little
2 = not much
3 = quite a lot
4 = a lot

(a) How much attention did you give them? Consider all distractions, such as looking away, looking at your phone, speaking to others, or thinking of something else.

(b) How much eye connection did you make? Consider actually looking into their eyes not just glancing and then looking elsewhere.

(c) How much listening did you do? Consider time spent rehearsing what you wanted to say next, interrupting them, not hearing some bits.

(d) How much energy did you put into the conversation? Consider how important what they said was to you, how enthusiastic you were, how much you were giving them, versus just being there.

(e) How much attention would the other person feel you gave them?

(f) How aware were you of what you looked like to them?

(g) How aware were you of what you sounded like to them?

(h) How much were your words congruent with your appearance and tone?

Results:

If you scored 24 to 32, that's fantastic – you are displaying intelligent leadership

If you scored 16 to 23, you are showing some signs of intelligent leadership

If you scored below 16, you still have some way to go

Most of us never score 32. We are familiar with being inside ourselves, rather than giving of ourselves. We think we converse well and that it is a simple skill. It isn't. Communication is difficult. But we take it for granted; we just do it and don't pay attention to it from moment to moment. We do it automatically, like driving to work each day.

To communicate well requires giving it the attention it deserves.

Think of it this way – a conversation is an instant coffee, effective communication is a freshly-ground, slow-filtered cappuccino. The first is fast and easy and tastes awful. The second takes care and effort and tastes supreme. Both contain coffee beans, but only one delivers.

In the book *Developing Management Skills*,[6] we outline attributes of supportive communication, which are useful here.

1.   Problem-oriented, not person-oriented.

'How can we solve this problem?'

Not: 'Because of you, there is a problem.'

2.   Congruent, not incongruent.

'Your behaviour really upset me.'

Not: 'Do I seem upset? No, everything's fine.'

3.   Descriptive, not evaluative.

'Here is what happened. Here is my reaction. Here is what I suggest would be more acceptable to me.'

Not: 'You are wrong for doing what you did.'

4.   Validating, not invalidating.

'I have some ideas, but do you have any suggestions?'

Not: 'You wouldn't understand, so we'll do it my way.'

5.   Specific, not global.

'You interrupted me three times during the meeting.'

Not: 'You're always trying to get attention.'

6.   Conjunctive, not disjunctive.

'Relating to what you just said, I'd like to discuss this.'

Not: 'I want to discuss this (regardless of what you want to discuss).'

7.   Owned, not disowned.

'I've decided to turn down your request because...'

Not: 'You have a pretty good idea, but they just wouldn't approve it.'

8.   Supportive listening, not one-way listening.

'What do you think are the obstacles standing in the way of improvement?'

Not: 'As I said before, you make too many mistakes. You're just not doing the job.'

MORE EMPATHY

You may have a 'good message', but without empathy that message can so easily be misheard, misunderstood, or mistaken. To be understood and influential, your message needs to impact with each person, according to their way of understanding, not yours.

Without emotional awareness your decisions are merely a cataloguing skill. Empathy allows emotional psychological inference about other person's mental states and feelings in social contexts. Being empathic is the gold star behaviour behind influential leadership. It means attentive, curious listening and observing – of yourself and the other person.

Influential leadership depends on the ability to truly understand and share the feelings of another person, and comprehensively convey that understanding by your demeanour, actions, and words. It is a busy, continuous process. Empathy is a continuous self-awareness process, not an accomplishment.

The good news is that empathy may be easier than we think.

CASE STUDY – PICK A CARD

In a study on empathy, participants reviewed images from two sets of cards. For one deck, they had to describe the physical characteristics of the person. For the other, participants had to feel empathy for the person in the photo—and also to guess their feelings.

Participants were told to choose freely between decks. Almost everyone picked the decks that didn't require feeling empathy, even for the photos of happy people. They consistently avoided connecting emotionally with strangers.

However, after people were told they were good at feeling empathy, their ability to see others dramatically increased. They started selecting more cards from the empathy deck. And they also reported that empathy required less mental effort than those who were told they weren't empathetic.

Some work relationships are simply transactional. It's a zero-sum game where both parties want to balance their gains and losses. The type of relationship needed for intelligent leadership is based on a mutual appreciation of the nature and qualities of both parties. This relationship can't last without trust, and that means empathy. Only by accepting others as they are can people be *mutually* influential. It takes more time and effort, but it is a richer deal.

Trust is an emotional expression, not a way of getting what we want. Trust starts and ends with the individual. It is who you are as a leader.

At a workplace level, a recent survey found that trustworthy leadership is a priority for employees when considering a place to work, above and beyond fair compensation, job security, culture and career advancement. However, only 32 per cent of employees felt that their company has trustworthy leaders.

Other findings revealed that one in five employees would be willing to work longer hours if they had leaders that they could trust. One in four stated they would extend their tenure if they trusted all levels of leadership to 'maintain transparency', and one in three indicated they would remain with the company longer if leaders 'kept their promises'.

In another survey of emotions at work, women were found to be more than twice as likely to cry in their workplace compared to their male colleagues (41 per cent versus 20 per cent). These numbers were reversed for emotional outbursts such as shouting or yelling.

59 per cent of respondents said they felt restricted in expressing their real emotions in the workplace at all, and 60 per cent said they would handle their own upsets, instead of seeking help from others.

This level of feeling (of being unable to express and discuss emotions at work) raises concerns about empathic leadership. To be effective in your workplace it is important to master your own development, truly understand your team, and manage the context of their workplace.

Emotions, power, and control are linked, which leads us now to looking at more ways of being empathic.

THE EMPATHIC LEADER'S CHECKLIST

Be a fantastic listener – Intense listening is vital to increasing empathy. To understand others, we need to let their stories flow, rather than try to impose our views or emotions. Start by not interrupting. Pay attention, take notes, and ask questions to show you care. Take the back seat. Let the other person drive. Don't force the pace or focus. Follow their lead. Avoid judging or criticising your employees for what they say. Create a safe space for trust and open communication.

Be enthusiastically present – Remove distractions. Make sure you are not checking the time or your phone when someone is sharing their struggles. Focus all your energy on being there. Make sure your mind is where your body is. We have the power to affect how others see us, and also how we see ourselves. Assuming body postures that convey competence and confidence, we change our cortisone and testosterone levels. This increases our ability to take risks and helps us perform better. Amy Cuddy in *Presence* writes in detail about being totally present.[7]

Work hard at understanding where the other person is coming from – Let go of right and wrong. Don't use your beliefs or thoughts to judge what the other person is telling you. Focus on understanding their perspective.

Create regular touchpoints – Building trust and rapport takes time and it is valuable in terms of an ongoing work relationship. Monitor how issues are evolving. Look for practical opportunities to connect and mark them. Make sure people feel that you are *always* ready to listen. Not just once.

Try not to give unsolicited advice – This is rescuing and demeaning. Some people will be looking for help. However, they need to ask for it, not just hint at it. Others just want to be listened to. Many people gain clarity simply by sharing their issues. Instead of giving advice, ask, 'What do you need from me? How can I help you?'

Encourage quiet voices – There are always a few people who take over meetings. Encourage participation by providing quiet voices the opportunity to speak up.

Get a coach – Becoming more empathetic is something that we can all learn and develop. An external coach can help you and your team become more aware. They can also provide a safe space and actionable tools for developing empathy across the whole group.

Lead with questions – Empathic leaders embrace intellectual humility. They welcome their vulnerable side—they want to bring out what is right, not be right. Good questions always access more discoveries than advice ever does. Explore the reasons why people are saying what they're saying. Getting to the root cause often reveals inconsistencies that require further thinking.

There may be times when you just don't feel like being empathetic. If this is the case, then don't have those crucial leadership conversations until you are in a better frame of mind to go through the steps outlined in the checklist. Wait for another day.

It is also important to remember that empathy is not a universal behaviour for all and any situation. A leader is not qualified to do counselling. That's why we have referrals to Employee Assistance Program (EAP) providers, coaches, psychologists, and other health professionals.

Empathy can be draining if not used selectively. Be empathic, but evaluate the person, context, and their reactions. If it feels uncomfortable or unsafe, be more protective of yourself. Choosing when and how to say no is also vital to successful leadership.

TIPS FOR HOW TO EMPATHETICALLY SAY NO

• Have a very clear set of principles about things that you will not do and will not agree to from the very beginning. Make a list of the

things that you will say no to, and those you would say yes to.
- Always follow your list.
- Ask clarifying questions before saying no.
- Provide a reason for saying no.
- Say no in a way that matches and mirrors the person making the request.
- If the 'no' could turn into a 'yes' in the future, identify what is required for this to happen.
- If you're saying no in order to delegate, make sure you provide what is needed the person to fulfil the role or complete the task.
- Say no if the only reason you want to say yes is to please someone.
- Say no with an equal opportunity policy. Don't have favourites to whom you say no and others to whom you always say yes.

DEVELOP YOUR EMPATHY

Step One: Perception
How you immediately perceive the other person is a guide to their perspective.

What do they appear like? Sound like? What's their job?

What do they really mean and think about the matter you are discussing? What are their perceptions and values about it? What do they need to hear to be receptive to you?

Gather as much verbal and non-verbal information as you can. What are their interests and job roles? What do they like and dislike? Do they read, watch TV, or travel? Learn as much about them as you can.

Note: check your biases and own agenda for false or biased perceptions.

Step Two: Adapt

Adapt your demeanour and communication to match their perspective.

Having the flexibility to adapt your communication style comes from engaging in lots of real-world practise and from extensive reading. The more you know about different sports, religions, hobbies, politics, and travel, the better your ability to match different perspectives. You don't have to have experienced everything first-hand in order to allude to understanding that perspective, you just need to be familiar with it.

So if someone plays or watches tennis, use the terminology of the game to communicate in a way that will resonate with them, such as, 'You aced that', or 'Good shot'. Or if someone reads biographies, use this information to tell them that you have always been interested in the life of a particular well-known figure that you admire.

You can start your empathy journey by practising on yourself. Do you value yourself as you are? Do you accept your feelings? If you are going to be empathic, you need to be honest, with yourself and others.

Neat rules for an empathic leader are to prepare, listen, speak little, speak last, and speak well.

EMPATHY QUESTIONNAIRE

This brief Emotional Intelligence (EQ) test from *Developing Management Skills*[8] will give you insight into your EQ before diving in deeper.

Your EQ determines your ability to understand and regulate emotions, and to continue to grow and develop emotionally. For this reason, EQ is widely regarded as the essential leadership quality.

Brief EQ Test

Finish each statement below by selecting the one answer that is most likely to be your response. Think about the way you usually respond to these kinds of situations. There are no right answers. However, it is easy to pick 'the best answer', rather than the one you believe would be your most likely response. Picking the 'best answer' rather than your genuine response will skew your results and you will not benefit from the test.

Mark only one answer per item.

1. When I get really upset, I...

(a) Analyse why I am so disturbed.

(b) Blow-up and let off steam.

(c) Hide it and remain calm.

2. In a situation in which a colleague takes credit in public for my work and my ideas, I would probably...

(a) Let it slide and do nothing, in order to avoid a confrontation.

(b) Later, in private, indicate that I would appreciate being given credit for my work and ideas.

(c) Thank the person in public for referencing my work and ideas, and then elaborate on my contributions.

3. When I approach another person and try to strike up a conversation, but the other person does not respond, I...

(a) Try to cheer up the person by sharing a funny story.

(b) Ask the person if he or she wants to talk about what is on his or her mind.

(c) Leave the person alone and find someone else to talk to.

4. When I enter a social group, I usually...

(a) Remain quiet and wait for people to talk to me.

(b) Try to find something complimentary I can tell someone.

(c) Find ways to be the life of the party or the source of energy and fun.

5. On important issues, I usually...

(a) Make up my own mind and ignore others' opinions.

(b) Weigh both sides and discuss it with others before making a decision.

(c) Listen to my friends or colleagues and make the same decision they do.

6. When someone that I do not particularly like becomes romantically attracted to me, I usually...

(a) Tell that person directly that I am not interested.

(b) Respond by being friendly but cool or aloof.

(c) Ignore the person and try to avoid him or her.

7. When I am in the company of two people who have diametrically opposing points of view about an issue (for example, politics, abortion, war) and are arguing about it, I...

(a) Find something about which they can both agree and emphasise it.

(b) Encourage the verbal battle.

(c) Suggest that they stop arguing and calm down.

8. When I am playing a sport and the game comes down to my last-second performance, I...

(a) Get very nervous and hope that I do not choke.

(b) See this as an opportunity to shine.

(c) Stay focused and give it my best effort.

9. In a situation in which I have an important obligation and need to leave work early, but my colleagues ask me to stay to meet a deadline, I would probably...

(a) Cancel my obligation and stay to complete the deadline.

(b) Exaggerate a bit by telling my colleagues that I have an emergency that I cannot miss.

(c) Require some kind of compensation for missing the obligation.

10. In a situation in which another person becomes very angry and begins yelling at me, I...

(a) Get angry in return. I do not take that from anyone.

(b) Walk away. It does not do any good to argue.

(c) Listen first, and then try to discuss the issue.

11. When I encounter someone, who has just experienced a major loss or tragedy, I...

(a) Really do not know what to do or say.

(b) Tell the person I feel very sorry and try to provide support.

(c) Share a time when I experienced a similar loss or tragedy.

12. When someone makes a racist joke or tells a crude story about a member of the opposite sex in mixed company, I usually...

(a) Point out that this is inappropriate and not acceptable, and then change the subject.

(b) Ignore it so I do not cause a scene.

(c) Get really upset and tell the person just what I think of what was said.

Scoring Key

The statements below are organised according to the key dimension of EQ being assessed. The numbers next to each answer indicate the number of points attached to that answer. Circle the alternatives you selected, and then add up the points for the twelve items.

Emotional awareness

1. (a) = 10
(b) = 0
(c) = 0

Explanation: Only answer a) indicates that you are aware of what is going on emotionally inside.

5. (a) = 5
(b) = 10
(c) = 0

Explanation: Answer a) may be okay if you are clear about your priorities, but answer b) indicates that you are aware of possible alternative points of view.

9. (a) = 0
(b) = 0
(c) = 10

Explanation: Only answer c) indicates that you are aware of your own emotional reactions and will require compensation for the inevitable upset it will create.

Emotional control (balance)

2. (a) = 0
   (b) = 5
   (c) = 10

Explanation: Answer c) implies that you are confident enough to handle the situation on the spot. Answer b) confronts the issue but not in the presence of those affected.

6. (a) = 10
   (b) = 5
   (c) = 0

Explanation: Answer a) is honest if it is done skilfully and avoids being harsh. Answer b) relies on the other person getting an indirect hint.

10. (a) = 0
    (b) = 0
    (c) = 10

Explanation: Only answer c) demonstrates emotional control.

Emotional diagnosis (empathy)

3. (a) = 5
   (b) = 10
   (c) = 0

Explanation: Answer a) may be appropriate in some circumstances, but answer b) indicates sensitivity to a possible emotional issue on the part of the other person.

7. (a) = 10
   (b) = 5
   (c) = 0

Explanation: Answer a) indicates an ability to recognise different emotions but to not get carried away by them. Answer b) acknowledges different emotional perspectives but may engender bad feelings or emotional casualties. Alternative c) does not acknowledge the different emotional commitments.

11. (a) = 0
    (b) = 10
    (c) = 0

Explanation: Only answer b) empathetically acknowledges the other person's feelings.

Emotional response

4. (a) = 0
   (b) = 10
   (c) = 0

Explanation: Answers a) and c) may indicate that you are not sensitive to the emotional climate of the group, and your behaviour may be inappropriate.

8. (a) = 0
   (b) = 5
   (c) = 10

Explanation: Answer b) may be appropriate if it is not a sign of narcissism, but answer c) is clearly an indication of emotional control.

12. (a) = 10
(b) = 0
(c) = 5
Explanation: Answer b) implies losing emotional control, whereas answer a) indicates remaining under control.
Your total score.....................
Comparison data mean score:
86 or higher = You have an extremely high EQ level
71–85 = You have a good EQ level
55–70 = You have a low EQ level
54 or lower = You have a very low EQ level

Self-Assessment

How did you go?

Put this score away and redo it again after completing the book and putting the suggestions into practise for several weeks. Note the changes in your overall score and on individual behaviours. The techniques in the test above are not complex. They just require your commitment to pay attention.

3

THE THREE-STEP LEADERSHIP CHANGE PROCESS

'Change your mind and come to your senses.'

– Zeig

In this chapter we will explore the importance of changing yourself to become a better leader. The method that we will be looking at is a three-step personal leadership change process, focused on overcoming competing beliefs.

The process requires a deep dive into your ways of thinking and behaving in the world. You are looking for all the values and behaviours that help you to successfully achieve your goals, and as well those that prevent this.

This change process combines leadership coaching with personal and organisational psychology. It is a safe, practical, and challenging approach, and you can work through it on your own.

From very early on in our lives we are immersed in a complicated and comprehensive training program to become who we are. For some this is a boot camp. For others it is a holiday.

In this period our personalities, beliefs, and behaviours are formed. In often paradoxical, but always intricate ways, we are bombarded with messages about ourselves, others, and the world. These messages are instilled by our primary caregivers, both verbally and non-verbally. We are frowned at, hugged, hit, sent to our rooms, ignored, smothered, cheered on, and so much more. Our primary caregivers teach us values, and model values. Often what we see modelled is not what we hear taught. It can often be a case of 'Do as I say, not as I do'.

Our amygdala can only handle a certain amount of data, so we selectively latch onto different bits of what we see and hear, and then we imitate those behaviours. This imitation of words, beliefs, and deeds is then reinforced by our caregivers, through either positive or negative verbal and non-verbal responses.

These behaviours are those that our caregivers took on as the way we should live. In the first five years we are submerged in this rich sea of nurturing and nagging – some of this we brush off and some bits attach themselves to us and shape who we are.

This is the foundation of how we develop our personalities and our behaviours, but it is not the complete story. Our personalities are not identical to our beliefs and behaviours, even if they are related. In the context of the three-step change process, we will be focusing on behaviours and values. Addressing aspects of personality is best done in therapy. Changing aspects of behaviour is suitable for coaching.

The bits of information that attach themselves to you form your beliefs and behaviours. This is your mental model, and you take it for granted. Your mental model supports you to be effective and successful, but also at times causes conflict and poor decisions. Some of your beliefs work in conjunction with each other, some conflict with each other.

So, your values and assumptions about yourself and the world, are taught and modelled by your primary caregivers. You adopt these beliefs unconsciously and adapt or reject them as you grow in knowledge and experience. By adulthood you have a fully formed set of rules about who you are and how other people are.

These beliefs shape partner choices, friendships, and how you get on in your world. They can ensure you have a satisfying and enjoyable life or an unsatisfactory and unhappy life.

You also bring these beliefs about how to behave into your leadership role. Yet there is a widely held belief that home and work are separate. This is why most leadership training doesn't work. Learning new leadership techniques does not change underlying behaviours and values.

Most adults don't have a clean slate of good decisions and attitudes. There are always a few limiting beliefs holding us back. Changing these unhelpful beliefs requires addressing old, underlying assumptions and making decisions that promote more successful behaviour.

In a leadership context, this is called reframing.[9] It is the case that some early assumptions get in the way of effective leadership behaviours, and it is helpful to replace or modify them with more effective beliefs.

You may be conscious of the beliefs that limit your effectiveness, yet you still hold onto them. These beliefs may not be very helpful, but they are very familiar. They may have worked for you to a certain extent. However, in order to improve your leadership skills, it is important to address these limiting beliefs. Which brings us to the process.

THE THREE-STEP LEADERSHIP CHANGE PROCESS

- **Step One**

    In Chapter One you made your decision about being an emotionally intelligent leader. In this step you will identify the behaviours that are helping achieve your decision and noting the behaviours that are preventing your decision from being achieved.

- **Step Two**

    Look at the beliefs that compete against or negate your Step One decision.

- **Step Three**

    Look at the assumptions that unconsciously drive your actions.[10]

Step One – Your Leadership Decision

Is your leadership decision from Chapter One still accurate and specific enough to give you a big step in the influential leadership direction? Modify it if you need to, and then write it down again.

EXAMPLE – LEADERSHIP STATEMENT

'My leadership decision is to build a culture of trust and honesty in the workplace.'

EXERCISE – STEP ONE LEADERSHIP STATEMENT

My leadership decision is to

....

....

....

In Chapter Two, you completed the empathy questionnaire. Reflect on your answers to the quiz and underline those behaviours that you can most easily use and develop further in the following months.

To help you get started, here are some suggestions of empathic behaviours.

Empathic behaviours:

- Being a good listener.
- Being kind.
- Being respectful.
- Valuing my colleagues.

Create sentences based on your own behaviours.

EXERCISE – EMPATHIC BEHAVIOURS

List your empathic behaviours here:

....
....
....
....
....
....

Also note those behaviours where you need more work. By committing to empathic leadership, you commit to developing these behaviours in your workplace. This is informed commitment. You are building your repertoire of empathic behaviours. Distinguish the behaviours that might have impeded you achieving empathic leadership, and give some thought to those that you have not been engaging in which may have helped in pursuing your goal.

To help you get started, here are some suggestions of non-empathic behaviours.

Non-empathic behaviours
- Becoming impatient.
- Disagreeing bluntly with the other person.
- Not thinking about the others' needs during conversations.
- Forgetting to match non-verbal cues.

Create sentences based on your own behaviours.

EXERCISE – NON-EMPATHIC BEHAVIOURS

List your non-empathic behaviours here:

....
....
....
....
....

Over the next four weeks, observe which of these behaviours help you to achieve your leadership decision, and which behaviours hold you back. Accentuate the helpful behaviours and reduce the ones that are holding you back.

Many excellent leadership decisions are corroded by a difficulty with taking full responsibility. You know what you want to do, but something holds you back from taking the risks required to achieve it. Truly responsible leaders cultivate self-awareness. This skill is crucial for spotting less mature decisions. Self-awareness builds empathy. There are many different means to achieving this—yoga, coaching, mindfulness, and feedback are a few popular ways. These methods are the introduction to revealing ourselves to ourselves. Even when you use these methods, you may still need to make the sometimes painful connections that create self-awareness on your own. Taking responsibility allows you to do this.

Awareness is usually about our emotional core, those deep feelings we wish to keep hidden. Many people avoid looking closely into the depths of their emotional core because it can seem as though it will be uncomfortable or downright scary. Therefore, it's good to wade into it from the shallow end, rather than diving off the highest board.

Your emotional core is made up of your beliefs, attitudes, and biases. Self-awareness involves considering why you have these beliefs, attitudes, and biases, and what you might do with them if you stopped hiding them away. The reason why you take the brave step of looking into your emotional core is in order to become a better leader and a better person.

Not taking responsibility involves making the following kinds of statements:

'It wasn't me, they did it.'

'The dog ate my homework.'
'She makes me so angry.'
'I can't help it.'
'If it wasn't for that, I would have succeeded.'
'You've hurt my feelings.'

EXAMPLE – NOW LOOK WHAT YOU MADE ME DO!

This example highlights how we reduce our influence by not owning our emotions. We are not acting responsibly.

Your colleague has made you angry. You were fine a minute ago, then they said that offensive thing, and the anger shot up inside you. As a result, you blame them for making you angry. Every inch of your experience confirms this.

Until you examine the experience.

1. You were feeling fine.

2. Your colleague said something that offended you.

3. You had an instantaneous anger reaction.

4. You yelled at them.

So the conclusion you draw is that they 'made' you angry. However, this reaction comes from your amygdala.

Prefrontal cortex analysis reveals:

1. They said something you decided was upsetting (they may or may not have intended to be offensive).

2. You generate a feeling of anger. It is your anger – no one else's. It occurred so quickly you weren't even aware that you created it. Nonetheless, it is *your* feeling. You are responsible for it, not your colleague.

You may have some resistance to this idea. It may go against your sense of what really happened. If this is the case, stay with this resistance for a little while. What exactly do you find uncomfortable about accepting that they did something, and you felt something? Why is it a struggle to believe they didn't *make* you feel something?

Overcoming your resistance to this idea puts you in charge of the things that you can control – your own feelings and actions. Being able to control your feelings and actions gives you the flexibility and capacity to respond to others much more influentially.

With this understanding, you can see that what actually happens is this:

1. Your colleague makes a comment. They are responsible for the comment, whether offence was intended or not. However, they are not responsible for your anger. That's all yours, possum.

2. You shift responsibility from you to them and react badly. As a result you, stop being influential.

Where's the accountability? Where's the chance to progress the relationship?

The first unconscious passive shift in blaming and not being accountable is often some version of, 'This is just the way I am'. Many of us have 'cherished' ways in which we blame others for our shortcomings. Think for a minute about your 'cherished' blame mantra.

Examples of some popular blame mantras:

'I just did what I was told.'

'There was no time for me to consider it properly.'

'They never listen.'

'I inherited that team.'

'I didn't want to cause offence.'

When you are clear about your most frequently repeated blame mantra, write it down.

EXERCISE – BLAME MANTRA

My cherished blame mantra is

....

....

....

Having written down your blame mantra, you have identified an area where you are not taking responsibility. You can now take this a bit further.

You are revealing the way your Step One decision is a sneaky way to avoid responsibility. By accepting that you have ownership of your beliefs, you give yourself the ability to succeed in changing your leadership behaviour. While our beliefs develop for our own self-protection over the years, we are usually unaware of this happening.

This takes us to your Step Two rules.

Step Two – Conflicting Decisions And Beliefs

This step takes you from blaming others to taking personal responsibility, allowing you to accept and manage that bit of the world you can control – yourself. It is your personal accountability measure. You may experience some internal resistance to this step.

EXAMPLE – CONFLICTING DECISIONS AND BELIEFS

The following example may help illustrate how our beliefs conflict with our primary leadership decisions.

In Step One, the example leadership statement read, 'My leadership decision is to build a culture of trust and honesty in the workplace.'

If you have the blame mantra, your Step Two decision may be 'People always take advantage of my good nature, so I will be a strong leader.'

The Step Two rule for you is in conflict with or impedes your influential leadership

This fear of upsetting people creates certain behaviours, such as not being able to say no.

This is where the conflict arises. The belief is that saying 'no' will upset people.

Holding the belief that saying no will upset people undermines the Step One leadership statement, 'My leadership decision is to build a culture of trust and honesty in the workplace.'

This is because a key element of building a culture of trust and honesty stems from being able to have difficult conversations. If this person always avoids upsetting people, then they cannot have difficult conversations and, therefore, they cannot build a culture of trust and honesty.

You develop many early assumptions about how you and the rest of the world *should* interact. Some of these are aligned with each other, and some are contradictory.

When your leadership decision conflicts with an early assumption, the more powerful of the two prevails. Frustratingly, that is usually the assumption, as this is a long-standing mantra and a cherished belief.

This means that your decision to be an honest and compassionate leader is a recent, and therefore less reinforced, commitment compared to your mantra of, 'Don't trust people.'

Your Step One decision and Step Two beliefs are inevitably in contradictory tension. Even when you genuinely want to achieve your Step One decision, your amygdala will work just as strongly to preserve your Step Two beliefs, as the amygdala thinks these beliefs are protecting you.

These countervailing pressures maintain a dynamic equilibrium that effectively keeps things pretty much as they are. Overcoming this contradiction can only occur when you recognise that it is *you* who is preventing change, even if it seems to be for good reasons.

This is the essence of accountability. No one 'makes' us feel or react in the ways that we do – our feelings and reactions result from our own beliefs. If we accept this, we accept we can change. If we refuse to take responsibility and blame others, we cannot change.

To help you get started, here are some examples of Step Two rules.

EXAMPLE – STEP TWO RULES

I must be seen as a strong leader.
I must not appear to be weak.
In order to be effective at work, I must not be distracted by 'people stuff'.

EXERCISE – YOUR STEP TWO RULES

My Step Two Rules are

....

....

....

....

Once you have worked out your Step Two rules, you can look at the assumptions that are connected with them.

Step Three – Changing Your Limiting Beliefs

In this step, you might consider some of your unquestioned long-standing assumptions about your nature and the ways you should behave. These are the beliefs you know are limiting your leadership. They may be uncomfortable to access, but they will not be overwhelming. If they were overwhelming, you would not be in a leadership role.

These assumptions take two forms:

Firstly, the ones you keep locked away, such as, 'I will never be very successful', 'It is important to be liked by everyone', and 'I'm really lazy'.

Secondly, the public mantras, such as, 'The strong survive', 'It is necessary to give 100 per cent every time', 'People are untrustworthy', and 'It's important to get in first'.

Whether your assumptions are locked away or proudly on display, they are limiting you.

Assumptions function as cognitive scripts that lead you to form belief statements about yourself, the motives of other people, and the world in which we live. These belief statements are often unconscious. They are your stories about who you are.

Dominant assumptions, such as 'the strong survive' can help you to thrive, and often lead to remarkable levels of success. However, they also govern how you interpret your world and, over time, they can become limiting and oppressive. In relationships, at work and at home, your assumptions can become templates that prevent you from truly being successful.

Your assumptions are the way you perceive and simplify reality. Your upbringing, education, religion, and life experience all shape your assumptions. It's how you handle the chaos of life, by having an automatic fixed position. Your mind is set, and this perspective determines how you will perceive and react to specific events.

Your assumptions can be beneficial or limiting. They may set you towards generosity and fairness, or form your biases and prejudices. Assumptions are often black and white and display a closed mindset. People will be perceived as trustworthy or not. Foreigners will be seen as a threat, or not. Money will be considered the root of all evil, or not. Hard work will be deemed to pay off, or not. Life will be viewed as fair, or not.

It can be seen that limiting assumptions, as the source of your biases and prejudices, impede or ruin your leadership skills. Conversely, beneficial assumptions provide you with a foundation for all your effective leadership behaviours.

Your assumptions are your internal code of conduct. This code of conduct is most strongly formed early in your life to enable you to please others and be accepted. Primarily, your assumptions are unconsciously learned by observation and imitation. Sometimes people develop assumptions that conform to their upbringing and culture, whereas other people may develop their internal code by rebelling against taught values.

For example, a family culture of 'put others first', may cause someone to adopt kindness and generosity. In its most negative form, this may lead to an over adaptive self-deprecation.

Alternatively, the same person may rebel against the family culture of putting others first, to become assertive or aggressively selfish. This early-developed rebellious code then may cause difficulties for a leader trying to achieve an open leadership style. Similarly, early compliance with the 'put others first' code may cause difficulties for a leader when tough work decisions are needed.

Sometimes these assumptions are rigid and remain unchallenged, or so strongly followed as to be firmly held convictions. Alternatively, some assumptions may be amended, reframed, or rejected, as you gain more knowledge and experience in your life. You may come to see the limitations of the particular worldview you were following and look at how you can accommodate a more nuanced way of being. This is connected to the way you develop and listen to your prefrontal cortex—your social brain. This flexibility is also formed by developing emotional intelligence.

You adopted your big assumptions early in life and then they slipped unnoticed into your leadership behaviours. You didn't question them. Either you were unaware of them, or if you did notice they were a little off, you may have polished them up to look more professional.

Your assumptions are an important part of your identity. If these assumptions are fairly positive then your leadership behaviours will also be fairly positive, and your skill development will be straightforward. If your assumptions are not so positive, then you will have more leadership development to do.

Here is an example of how early, unexamined assumptions might morph into leadership behaviours.

EARLY ASSUMPTIONS	LEADERSHIP BEHAVIOURS
I'm not good enough.	I'll show them who's boss.
The world is unsafe.	I will not trust anyone.
I like sharing my things.	I am an inclusive leader.
I always screw up.	I will get everything perfectly right.
I must always be nice to people.	I will avoid difficult conversations.
I must not miss out.	I am a micro-manager.
I am not very special.	I must question my leadership.
I am so special.	I am the greatest leader.
I must think of others.	I will be a considerate leader.

There are a number of ways we reinforce our big assumptions.

1. We tell stories to ourselves and others about our assumptions. Then we believe our own stories – and others may, too. This reinforces the assumptions we have made and the identity we have created.

2. We know our assumptions are right. This feeling of certainty is actually **confirmation bias.** This means we stop listening if people and data contradict what we believe.

3. We share the assumptions others have taught us. People have a strong need to be in agreement with others. The tribe protects us, and intra-group conflict is a personal threat. The amygdala triggers a pain response to threat, and so we grab at agreement. This ancient protective response can stop us from exploring better and more complex options. If we do explore other options, and disagree very strongly with the tribe, then we may join a new tribe.

4. We have a deep desire for control. Control is illusory at best and destructive at worst. However, in the short-term, it makes us feel good and staves off the anxiety of having to take risks.

You can break down your assumptions and develop greater self-awareness by asking yourself three vital questions.

1. Why do I believe what I believe? People often confuse their assumptions with the truth, and rarely question how they came to hold them. To break this pattern, stop looking for evidence to support your assumptions and instead try looking for the sources of those beliefs. For example, did they come from an external authority, such as your parents or teachers? As you examine your system of beliefs, you might find your belief that 'loyalty is supreme' was inherited from your father's modelling and parental messages, because loyalty mattered most to him.

2. Might I be wrong or mistaken? Question yourself. Consider that there may be other ways of seeing the world that are just as useful. For example, in the case of the belief that 'loyalty is supreme', consider broader contexts and other types of loyalty, and you may find how blind loyalty can lead to poor outcomes in certain cases.

3. How do I want to be viewed in the future? This question is not about what you want to do next or what your career path will be. It is about considering who you will be next. What image would you like to embrace?

Fight or flight was the best option early in the history of humanity, but the modern world is changing faster than our brains can evolve. Assumptions that once helped us make life-saving decisions quickly are not as crucial as they once were. As a result, working on reframing your beliefs will enhance your prefrontal lobe and manage your amygdala.

The challenge is, how do you change your major limiting assumptions in order to be a more empathic leader?

It is not straightforward, for the simple reason that the ways in which your early assumptions developed can actually prevent you from changing them. To ensure lasting change, you need to reach outside yourself and remodel your belief system. This can be especially hard if you are addressing a mental model of the world that you believe is your safety net.

Common phobias might demonstrate this dilemma. If you have developed a strong understanding that heights are dangerous, and you reinforced this anxiety with several unsafe height experiences during your life, you may well develop a fear of heights. With your assumption driving your phobia, no amount of persuasion will convince you otherwise. You need to go back and reconstruct the building blocks of your original understanding. Your early observing and instruction need to be re-evaluated with an external objective mindset. Your early decision to avoid heights at all costs requires a 're-decision' which classifies a range of height scenarios that have different levels of danger.

You may have had a phobic parent who panicked whenever they were on a hill or bridge. You may have stumbled near a cliff edge, and this may have drawn a frantic reaction from your parents. You may have crossed a stream on an unsteady bridge and fallen off. And so on.

You had a wealth of data that taught you heights are dangerous. From this data, you made the assumption that all heights are dangerous. This would have led you to unconsciously decide, 'I will avoid all heights. They are dangerous.' This is a fight/flight fixed response. Objectively, heights are on a continuum, from very safe to very dangerous.

For example, wide mountain roads with strong barriers, well-built bridges, and ascending a tall structure in a modern lift are all very safe and require little or no fear. Conversely, narrow mountain hiking trails, unstable bridges, rickety ladders, and climbing over sloping roofs are good to avoid. Even so, although they are good to avoid, you don't require fear to prevent you from avoiding them.

To change your thinking, you need some way to re-examine your original assumption and observe how it was based on very little evidence. You trusted your parent without question. You had bad experiences with heights. You ignored safe examples of crossing bridges in cars and maintained your fear. Using more of your prefrontal cortex and keeping your amygdala under wraps, you might re-examine height in all its forms.

Changing requires recognising and accepting objective reality as something distinct from your way of shaping reality. A very simple example of this is the perspective shock of driving a car for the first time in a foreign land. The steering wheel is on the *wrong* side!

How To Fill In Step Three

Start by reviewing what you have written in your Step Two rules. This is a key to your assumptions.

If there is a negative in your Step Two rules, for example, if your Step Two rule is 'I'm committed to not appearing to be weak', modify the words to form a sentence like this: 'I assume that if I were to be seen as weak then...'

If there is no negative in your Step Two, for example, if your Step Two is, 'I must be seen as a strong leader', then create a negative wording, to form a sentence like this: 'I assume that if I am not seen as a strong leader then...'

Assumptions generally take a form that reveals a fear. For example:

'I assume that if I am not seen as a strong leader, then I would be a failure yet again.'

'I assume that if I am not seen as being productive at work then I will be fired.'

There are as many mental models as there are people. These mental models are built from our assumptions, and they are all logically convincing in stopping us from being fully responsible and accountable.

EXAMPLE – ASSUMPTIONS

'I assume that if I really did make time to try to act on my goal, then I'd discover I actually can't do it.'

'I assume that if I really did have difficult conversations, then no one would like me.'

'I assume that if I refused to listen to gossip about a colleague, then I will be seen as rude.'

It is important to note that if you have an assumption such as, "I assume that if I disagree with my boss then I will never be promoted' that you don't replace this limited, closed mindset with an equally unhelpful open mindset. *Remember objective reality.* Use your street smarts, wisdom, intelligence, and EQ to distinguish which bosses you can safely disagree with, and those who may react badly. As with the example of heights, letting go of the fear doesn't always mean that every situation will be safe.

Once you have filled out one of your Step Three assumptions, you might complete this process with two or three other Step Two rules, in order to have a more comprehensive picture of your mental model.

The thing that holds most people back from getting to where they want to go is that their lives are being shaped by the stories they tell themselves. But no one else cares about your story or your assumptions. They respond to you according to how you behave to them.

Putting Your Leadership Statement Into Practice

- Discuss your leadership statement with your partner and closest friends.
- Observe yourself in relation to your assumptions. Notice and keep notes of what does or does not occur as a consequence of holding onto your limiting assumptions.
- Actively look for experiences that contradict your limiting assumptions. Collect data. Discuss this evidence with people who can take an objective view.
- Explore the history of your assumptions. Assumptions usually take root when we are little and very dependent on bigger brains. Consider what you didn't know and understand then that you do know and understand now.
- Conduct safe, simple tests about your assumptions. Test out your experiences and

thoughts with friends, a leadership coach, or a counsellor. As you get more confident ask trusted co-workers if they have noticed any changes in your leadership style. Appreciate your efforts on this.

Adjusting, modifying, and addressing your Step Three limiting assumptions will solidify your Step One decision.

YOUR THREE-STEP LEADERSHIP TEMPLATE

Step One
My leadership commitment is
....
....
....
....

My helpful behaviours are
....
....
....
....

My restricting behaviours are
....
....
....
....

Step Two

My rules are

....
....
....
....

Step Three
My limiting assumptions are

....
....
....
....

I will actively modify my limiting assumptions by

....
....
....
....

EXAMPLE – GRAHAM'S THREE-STEP LEADERSHIP PROCESS

Step One
My Leadership Statement:
'I decide to be the best leadership coach by giving support that is strong and creates change.'
My helpful behaviours are:
1. Having clever ideas.
2. Genuinely caring for others.

3. Being inquisitive.

My restricting behaviours are:

1. Giving too much instruction and direction.

2. Being a perfectionist.

3. Avoiding giving hard feedback.

4. Doubting myself.

Step Two

My Step Two Rules:

I must be nice and help people.

I must not get things wrong.

Step Three

My limiting assumptions are:

I assume that if I'm not always nice then...

I am not a nice person.

I will be left alone.

I assume that if I get things wrong then...

I will be shamed forever.

I will not be able to face people again.

I will actively modify my assumptions by:

Understanding that I like spending time on my own.

Understanding that being liked by everyone is not possible or needed.

Understanding that shame is not needed, and that mistakes are there for learning and growth.

This process took some time, and real discomfort, to work through.

Looking at my behaviours after three months I noticed the Step Two behaviours listed in my

Three-Step Leadership Process stood out amongst a host of others. I was too focused on solving problems *for* leaders and not *with* them. It wanted perfect results for my clients. Occasionally I avoided a blunt observation in favour of being nice. And I wanted to work in the session, not waste time on connecting and sharing. I was curious and clever so that was nice.

I unearthed a competing belief that involved being nice and helping others in a rescuing way. This was compounded by another strong belief – that it was not okay to be wrong.

I recalled the early occasions on which felt I needed to be nice. It was when I was young and learnt stuff like, 'Pride goes before a fall', and, 'Don't upset the neighbours'. The punishment for these sins was being shut in a room on my own.

As a result, I made a mantra of, 'When you're not nice you end up alone'. This mucked up my leadership decision. So I embarked on some reframing and new perspective efforts. This had me challenging what 'not being a nice person' meant. I used the continuum approach, with Hitler at one end and Nelson Mandela at the other end. I actually rated pretty well, somewhere up the good end. This continuum method was very helpful in contrast to my previous binary, 'Either you are a bad person or you are a good person', approach.

I then explored what being alone meant in real life, and historically. The conclusion was that in my life now, being alone was a choice, not an imposition. In fact, I often chose to be alone, because I find it pleasant.

Now I make interventions by trusting my experience. If I do unintentionally upset someone by giving hard feedback, rather than panicking that they will not like me, I can talk things through with them.

CASE STUDY – THE THREE-STEP LEADERSHIP EXERCISE

A six-partner law firm identified that they did not always follow agreed policies, and this was causing client annoyance and internal conflict.

The best approach seemed to be for them to carry out the Three-Step Leadership exercise as a group.

Their Step One leadership statement was 'We decide to adhere to the firm's policies.'

Step Two revealed that each of the six partners thought their way of doing things was the best way. Although they all had different ideas about what the best way was, the competing belief had a common theme, namely, 'My way is best'. This undermined their Step One leadership statement, and so they agreed to call each other out when they observed any 'my way is best' behaviour.

The two founding partners of the law firm had taken an entrepreneurial approach to their business, creating a culture of individualism. As the company grew and more partners came on board, the infrastructure became more complex, with a greater number of policy procedures. We clarified that although they had addressed this compliance with rules, they had not changed the underlying culture.

Step Three, which they shared openly with each other, showed a variation of self-created stories about being a failure if they didn't assert themselves strongly.

The result of the comprehensive Three-Step leadership assessment was that the partners embarked on a cultural change process.

SUMMARY OF THE THREE-STEP LEADERSHIP CHANGE PROCESS

- Commit to developing your emotionally intelligent leadership.
- Reflect and note all your behaviours that do not support your commitment.
- Reflect and note any behaviours that you could engage in that would support your commitment.
- Using these last two observations, deduce what your competing commitment might be.

- Explore where the competing commitment comes from. Identify the historical assumption that drives your resistance to becoming a truly emotionally intelligent leader.
- Let go of the assumption and overcome the resistance.

You have now committed to make a personal change so you can be a more influential leader. This is what true leadership is about.

Next, we will move on to interconnected techniques that you can use to reinforce the changes you are making. These techniques are the six supporting skills of the mirror method.

These skills are interconnected and overlapping. Each is important. Some will be more suited to you than others, and more applicable in some situations than in others. Moreover, they are experiential skills – the more you practise them, the more you develop and expand your repertoire.

The six skills are:

Matching – how to mirror non-verbal signs so you will be familiar and trustworthy as a leader.

Influencing – how to mirror their unique communication patterns and increase your connection.

Respecting – how to value yourself and the other person to develop safety and trust.

Reframing – how to show things in a different light so new solutions become available.

Observing – how to listen and learn to increase your understanding as a leader.

Reflecting – how to prepare, monitor and consolidate your message for best impact.

These skills enable your influence to be applied in every leadership context.

4

MATCHING

'It's not the notes you play, it's the notes you don't.'

– Miles Davis

We have established that effective communication depends upon being recognisable to the other person as safe and familiar. **Matching** is how you do this.

Matching is about imitation and connection. It primarily focuses on the spaces, pauses, frowns, gestures, and smiles that take place in a conversation, rather than the words. Matching is the 'unplayed notes'.

Matching is how we first learn to live in this world. The matching skill is how we learn from others, and transfer our learning to them.

Evolutionarily, Homo sapiens matched the tribe. Modern humans consciously and unconsciously match their friends, pets, and partners.

Business leaders, on the other hand, do not naturally match with their teams. Their natural inclination to fit in is overshadowed by the need to be busy and 'important'.

However, it is possible to consciously and deliberately match with your counterpart in order to build the work relationship and achieve your organisational goals. Matching is a motivating leadership skill, not just a way of being someone's buddy. It's nice for leaders to be liked. It is important for leaders to achieve their aims. With matching, you can have both.

Step one of great matching: **observation.**

Understand the context and the mood before you speak. Pay attention to the pauses, eye movements, tone of voice, body adjustments, and so on. Be curious. All these non-verbal signals are telling you something. This type of leadership says 'we are on the same team' without saying it out loud.

Leadership by matching tells the other person you belong to the same tribe, that you share the same values and believe in the same things. You don't have to pretend to belong. You simply need to match the other person's non-verbal behaviours.

CLASSIC VISIBLE MATCHING MOMENTS

Picture these images:

1. A happy mother and her newborn baby. The loving smiles that join them in a nurturing bubble, their faces nearly touching each other.

2. A fight between a teenager and a parent. The angry shouting and gesticulating from opposite sides of the room.

3. A young couple in love. The long, lingering gazes into one another's eyes.

4. A sports team after a victory. The tightly joined circle of people embracing and shouting out the team's song.

These are all examples of what matching looks like.

WHAT, WHEN AND HOW TO MATCH

Matching is entirely focused on appearing familiar, safe, and trustworthy. It is mostly a non-verbal process. The more familiar or similar you are to the other person, the more you will be seen as trustworthy and influential.

We feel safe with what we like, and unsafe with things that are unfamiliar. This bisects race, gender, and age. However, you can skilfully match even when there is an obvious disparity.

This is achieved in ways such as adults squatting down to a child's level in order to talk to them, or a manager not interrupting a voluble colleague, or someone admiring a painting on their friend's wall even if they don't know anything about modern art. We all tend to imitate quite naturally without paying attention to it.

Matching is respectful, intentional imitation.

Internally, and with your whole demeanour, this means treating the other person *fully* as your equal. Think about that. How often do you consider that quality when you are having a big conversation? How often do you have a default position that everyone is your equal? Think of your last contact with a client's executive assistant.

Matching requires a genuine wish to connect and to learn.

CASE STUDY – MATCHING

I was facilitating some executive development with a senior vice president. His CEO had requested that he see me, in order to help him manage his hyper-energy problem. He bounced into my office, flung himself into a chair and said, 'Well let's get to it, then', before instantly leaping back out of the chair and prowling my office.

I instantly decided my office wasn't big enough for both of us, and suggested we go for a walk in the nearby park. He was causing me to feel hectic and pressured. I chased him out of the office and across the road to the park. I started matching him by running at his pace. After a few minutes I 'accidentally' dropped my keys on the ground and stopped to pick them up. This induced him to stop, too. Then I resumed walking at a brisk pace, but less than the pace we were going before. He stayed with me.

My thoughts also slowed down a bit. A while later I invited him to look at a particularly interesting tree. When we resumed walking we were now walking at my normal pace. We talked quietly on our leisurely return to my office.

That was my matching him, and him matching me. Not only did we become synchronised in terms of our pace but also in terms of our focus and calmness of mind. After a more relaxed second session we spent some time discussing his assumption that if you slow down you will always be overtaken and left behind.

That is mirroring.

Current research demonstrates that, just like verbal messages, non-verbal communication has physical and vocal characteristics. Where verbal sounds denote the content of the message, non-verbal sounds refer to the manner in which the message is conveyed.

This includes both visible and audible cues, delivered with the message content. Each fragment of non-verbal behaviour has the potential to communicate meaning. All the conscious, subconscious, or unconscious non-verbal cues transmitted have an immense impact on the overall message conveyed.

This means that having precise awareness of your own cues, and the other person's, along with the ability to effectively utilise these cues, will build strong connections and influence.

Alongside your words, your demeanour, gestures, facial expressions, and tone of voice are ways you can match the person you are speaking with. Lots of evidence supports the fact that words are only a small part of the impact of your communication. The more skilfully you use matching, the more both of you create a shared communication. Out of this shared communication evolves a shared understanding. As though you both arrived at the conclusion together. This is non-verbal empathy.

Skilful matching depends upon your ability to observe and listen. It is like an echo between two people, creating a favourable impression in the mind of the person you are matching.

Recall the discussion about how your brain becomes overloaded with too much data, so that you unconsciously, selectively, generalise when you are talking to someone. You will see a tiny expression or gesture, make a categorisation, and stop seeing.

It is worth asking yourself how often do you really look at face of the person you are conversing with. When is the last time you were absorbed by someone's face when you were speaking with them? Try it today. What did you notice? Do their eyes narrow? Is their frown deep, modest, or suggestive? Are their lips still, always moving, pursed, or tight?

MATCHING AND UTILISATION

Utilisation involves using whatever response the other person offers you, verbal or non-verbal, and twisting it in a positive way. You utilise the person's existing frames or scripts to mobilise the resources and skills they already possess, or to deflect their criticism.

If they are religious you can ask, 'What does the Bible say about that?'

If they argue you can say, 'You don't agree? What it is that you believe?'

If they are silent you can say, 'You seem to be thinking seriously about this.'

Use everything that you know about yourself and the other person to make the conversation familiar and aligned. Harness your tone and presentation. Assume that the other person might know something you don't. Then discover what it is.

Appearing to be familiar to the other person is the fundamental aspect of trust. There is a neurological safety in being similar and non-threatening. It also enables you to better accept and recognise the other person.

You can get in tune, be connected, empathic, and understood, through matching these six areas:

1. Context

Prepare for your significant conversations beforehand. Think about the conversation from their point of view, rather than yours. Consider what do you know about them. Research them online, and ask colleagues about what might they think and feel. What is the history behind this upcoming conversation?

What is the topic of your conversation? Is this a matter they would feel is best discussed in their office or yours? Maybe they would feel more comfortable at a café, or on a walk? COVID has made this context matching quite limited but see the next chapter on Influencing.

Be in a good mood and smile. Being grumpy doesn't help you match with anyone in a positive way.

2. Worldview

Be widely read and informed about lots of stuff, so you can link your teaspoonful of knowledge about a topic with their ocean of experience. What do you know about their politics, habits, and attitudes about the world? You don't have to embrace these attitudes in order to show understanding of them.

You can match a politically right-of-centre person with comments about tradition, principles, or values. Alternatively, you can match a left-leaning person by noting resistance to change or the state of the world.

If they travel extensively, you can ask about places they've been that you've read about or visited. If they have young children, you can ask whether their child has reached the stage of asking 'why' all the time.

EXERCISE – WORLDVIEW

Pick a person you need to have an important conversation with. Research them and/or consider what you know about them. Write five subtle matching worldview comments you could use with them if the opportunity arises.

1

....

....

....

2

....

....

....

3

....

....

....

4

....

....

5

In the same way young children learn language through things that are familiar and comfortable, we take on new ideas and information best when they are presented in familiar and recognisable ways.

Where you do genuinely share someone's worldview this is easy. If you don't favour their worldview, consider that you won't change it by disagreeing with them or presenting them with facts. It is very unlikely that you will change someone's or biases and prejudices through scientific facts and evidence.

The point is that you don't have to agree with someone else's worldview or change your own worldview in order to use this as a tool for matching. You simply need to present yourself in a way that is compatible with their worldview.

By knowing the nature of the person and being thoughtful, you are better able to shape the way you present yourself to them. This means that, at the very least, there will be no clash of values, and at the very best, there will be a comfortable integration of values and views.

3. BODY LANGUAGE AND TONE OF VOICE

In this context, body language and tone of voice refer to all the ways we send messages about our feelings without speaking. Our facial expressions, grimaces, smiles, and frowns, how we dress, stand, or sit, how we move our arms or keep still, and all our gestures.

Tone of voice can be sharp, harsh, soft, loud, modulated, or staccato. Observing and listening carefully will reveal these non-verbal expressions.

Matching body language and tone of voice are commonly used techniques in acting workshops. One person acts a part with an emotion such as anger, fear, or joy, and another person will do their best to match their verbal and non-verbal behaviour. Done well the person who is doing the matching begins to *feel* the emotion.

The ability to match body language and tone of voice is important in influential communication. Body language and tone of voice are a direct representation of all of our emotions. There are the not-so-hidden signals, such as crying when sad, gritted teeth when angry, laughing when happy, and widening the eyes when scared.

There are hundreds of more subtle examples of the correspondence between our feelings and our bodies, which are dependent on our culture and upbringing.

You do not have to learn lots of these examples to be effective at matching emotional body signals. Regardless of what someone's body might be saying, you simply match them.

Only two things are needed. The first is a knowledge of your own emotional body signals. The second is the ability to match the other person's emotional body signals.

In this way you don't 'read' the nature of their feelings, you simply mirror them. This is respectful communication, not judgemental. Knowing your own subtle non-verbal messages enables you to prevent unhelpful signals that you might otherwise display without being aware of them.

Neuroscience research using physical skin conductance level, heart rate, and subjective emotional responses was measured against a set of consistently agreed feelings. There was a direct correlation between fear, anger, and the physical measures. These experiments further established the crucial role of our old friend, the amygdala, in picking up the emotional cues and selecting the immediate response.

Further research also confirmed the role of the prefrontal cortex in moderating and guiding the fight/flight reaction of the amygdala. The face, voice, and whole of body expressions inform a large part of the message. In fact, as we will see in a few pages, using non-verbal communication in a matched way is a vital element in effective connection.

It is worth noting that you need to incorporate as much information as possible into your analysis of someone's body language. Early in my career I had a technique-changing confrontation with the idea that you could read body language.

I had read a book called *Read Peoples' Body Language*, which purported to explain that different postures revealed secret feelings in others. Amongst other things the author stated that arms crossed in front of the chest signalled anger.

I was having a counselling session with an unruly twelve-year-old who was firmly clenching his arms in front of himself and speaking in monosyllables.

'Hmmm', I said, with smug superior knowledge, 'Why are you so angry?'

'Watcha talkin bout?' he replied.

'Well, when you cross your arms like that it means that you're angry.' I explained.

'Bullshit. It's bloody cold in here.'

I never used body language in that way again.

In communicating with your counterpart, here are a few ways in which you might match their body language.

- If they stand in a very upright posture, do the same.
- If they are very relaxed, be floppy.
- If they gesticulate a lot, use your hands when you talk.

- If they make eye contact, meet their gaze.
- If you know they dress very well, then dress up a bit. If they go for jeans and t-shirts, dress down a bit.

You may worry that if they notice what you are doing then they will think you are making fun of them. If you are clumsy and too obvious in your matching then this is possible.

However, just because *you* know what you're doing doesn't mean *they* will. Surprisingly, most people don't pick up on it at all. This is definitely true if your intention is to connect empathically and not manipulatively.

Even so, it is good to be a little subtle and sophisticated in your imitation. If they use lots of arm and hand gestures, make some small movements with your arms and hands, but not as frequently as they do. If they keep a lot of physical distance between the two of you, don't crowd them. Note their general demeanour and match it.

Now the voice...

Listen. Listen without labelling. Notice and reject your shudder at those voice tones that sound like your nagging aunt. Listen to how this person sounds.

If they speak really quickly, speed up the pace of your own speech a little. If they use lots of pauses, then put spaces between your sentences. Some people whisper, some people shout. Match these volumes subtly. Note if there is a rising inflection at the end of their sentences or a falling inflection. Pay attention to the patterns of their speech, and match it.

Interestingly, voice tonality that conveys negative emotions is perceived as significantly louder than tonalities that are neutral or positive in tone, even when they have the same amplitude.

4. BELIEFS AND VALUES

What we believe in is who we are. Our beliefs dictate our reality. The purpose of this way of matching is not to change your beliefs and values. It is about understanding the other person's perspective, and gaining insight into how they might have formed their beliefs and values. Learn about them and their interests. Use small talk to share some of your interests and see what that elicits. Find something about their position that you can appreciate, and recognise that aspect of their beliefs and values.

5. MEANING

People don't always say what they mean, and don't always do what they say. So how do we understand what other people mean? And how can others know what we mean?

As we've just seen, one important way of gaining this insight is to match the other person's body language as comprehensively and consistently as possible. This helps you get inside the nature and meaning of their perspective.

The second important way to gain this insight is to ask questions about what they mean, rather than assuming that the meaning is clear.

One effective way of doing this is to repeat back a fragment of the other person's last sentence.

Person A: 'I am so annoyed with Kim, she's so confusing.'

Person B: 'You find her confusing?'

Person A: 'Well, more aggravating.'

Person B: 'How does that feel?'

Person A: 'Actually I feel hurt by it.'

Person B: 'If you are hurt, what do you need to do about it?'

The third element of this is to identify the fundamental emotion behind the message, which may not be the same as the displayed emotion. By asking questions that match their message, you can uncover the meaning underlying that message and learn what their real concerns are.

We all implicitly attach meanings to different behaviours based on own biases and prejudices. We then (often inaccurately) ascribe these meanings the other person's behaviour.

For example, when I'm interrupted, I immediately feel the other person is being thoughtless or rude. I attach a critical meaning to a neutral behaviour.

EXERCISE – ATTRIBUTING MEANINGS

Think about some of the meanings you attribute to other people's behaviour and make a list of those meanings:

....
....
....
....
....
....
....
....

6. EXPECTATION

Expectation can be predicted and matched. When you are about to meet someone, think about what they might be expecting from you. How do they expect you to be dressed? How do they expect you to present yourself?

Developing an expectant attitude in yourself and others is powerful influencing. When our unspoken expectations are largely met we develop trust and agreement. When our expectations are contradicted we tend to close off and be uncertain. The nice thing about matching expectations is that you can often ask people directly what it is they are expecting.

For example, 'In terms of our discussion next Tuesday, what sorts of things are you hoping to get?' Or, 'Is my suggestion meeting your needs?' Questions such as these can help you shape and fine-tune your understanding of the other person's expectations and therefore meet them more appropriately.

FAMILIARITY

We all naturally accommodate to the group we are in, and in most cases we join groups that fit in with us. As individuals we tend to mirror our partners, colleagues, and pets.

I have some cute photos of owners and their pets where the mirrored similarity is striking.

Matching consists of mirroring others in a considered and specific manner. This builds a sense of safety, furthers understanding and develops clarity of meaning. Although we are all individuals, as we communicate with others we create a shared reality. This shared reality involves the words that are spoken, as well as the things that are not spoken of directly, and it lets people see themselves and each other more clearly.

Genuine connection depends upon matching and observing. If you develop this one trait, you can create a personal connection with anyone.

Emails and social media are now dominating our methods of communicating. Complex emojis and gifs are used, to enhance communication. However, in spite of the thousands of emojis and gifs that are available to help us communicate electronically, personal connection in face-to-face settings remains the best empathy builder.

In my consulting experience, too many messages are conveyed by social media and too few by face-to-face chats. This is particularly an issue when it comes to messages about downsizing, mergers, and other significant organisational changes. And yet people continue to wonder why communication is rated as a major issue in most staff surveys.

Written words lose the non-verbal messaging. With face-to-face you can see the impact of what you are saying and adjust, clarify, and amend. It is affirming and validating. It is a two-way engagement, not a one-way publication.

Face-to-face connection isn't something anyone should be willing to lose. Whether you're giving a presentation or making friends in a bar, your ability to connect is something other people can sense. It's what makes you memorable and magnetic. Employers and recruiters have known this for years. It is the reason why soft skills such as listening and communication are often prized over technical skills.

The important point to understand is that everyone wants to be seen and heard. More than this, everyone has a story to tell. If you can find how you connect with their story, you won't have to force the connection, you'll actually be present, and the other person will be aware of this.

When looking for how you connect with someone else's story, it is good to remember that nothing is inherently interesting or boring.

Your perspective is what determines your interest, or lack of it. Keeping this in mind gives you the opportunity to always have positive interactions.

EMPATHIC MATCHING

When someone latches onto a person or an idea, they want to engage more closely. There are a few ways to make it easier for people to engage with you.

1. Don't put up walls

If you're talking to an engineer about his job and the first words out of your mouth are, 'Oh I hate maths' then the conversation is over before it even started.

On the other hand, staying open allows you to find value in someone else's hobbies and skills. As long as you don't put up any walls, there's always an opportunity to steer the conversation into shared territory.

2. Meet people halfway

Not everyone you talk to is going to become a great buddy. In fact, you probably won't have all that much in common with most of the people you meet.

Going back to the conversation with the engineer, if he starts talking about the all the details of a structure he's building then, unless you are also an engineer, you are likely to quickly feel lost. However, if you enquire a little more deeply, you are likely to find some common ground. You will be able to pinpoint something that interests both of you.

EXAMPLE – FINDING COMMON GROUND

I was coaching the Chair of the Equestrian Federation Australia. Before our first meeting I was scratching my head, trying to identify some common ground, given horses are just not my thing.

As a communication expert I decided it would be interesting to explore how riders communicate with their horses. After a few opening words, I asked, 'When a horse approaches a hurdle, how do you communicate exactly when to jump?'

I was a friend for life. With just one sentence I had created empathy and trust. By meeting at the point where her work and mine overlapped I was able to open an empathic, influential conversation.

3. See each conversation as an opportunity

Be curious about the possibilities in every conversation you have. Even (maybe especially) at work, be open to asides that may open up new familiarities and ways to increase your influence.

TIPS AND IDEAS FOR MATCHING

1. People don't respond to what others say, they respond to the way it is said. So pay attention to your tone of voice and body language.

2. Saying something the way someone else expects to hear it helps you to be understood. Be as aware as possible of their expectations and deliver your message matching their expectancy.

3. Positive feelings help focus our understanding, negative feelings confuse our understanding. You are able to be strongly empathic when you are in a positive frame of mind. If you are not in a good frame of mind, wherever possible, delay your important conversations.

4. Accept that you don't always say what you mean, and you don't always mean what you say. Allow that sometimes, despite your

best intentions, some ideas don't get conveyed as you wish. Where this happens, apologise.

5. The more important something is to you, the less you will be understood. This is a great and unexpected obstacle to empathic connection. Holding something as a big deal in your conversation makes it too personal and imposing. Your passion overshadows your message, so that the meaning gets lost behind your intensity.

6. What you expect is what you tend to get. If you expect to have a positive conversation, you will.

7. When you treat the other person with respect, understanding flourishes.

The essence of every influential conversation, particularly difficult ones, is to share knowledge in a comfortable, trustworthy relationship with a person you like or feel affinity with. Being focused on the goal to the exclusion of being present is poor matching.

When you provide someone with new data, they quickly accept evidence that confirms their existing beliefs, and assess counterevidence with a critical eye. The mind seems to happily adopt opinions most convenient to its established views. With this in mind, it is worth considering how the other person's existing outlook can help clarify the way in which you present arguments that will be most convincing to *them,* rather than most convincing to *you.*

At the root, as humans, we identify more with the person we're facing if we perceive them as being like us. By tuning into the other person, you can be effective in your conversation. The way you communicate will influence, and be influenced by, the way the other person communicates.

The same significance can be assigned to your body in context of the way you produce verbal and non-verbal cues. In verbal communication you only use vocal organs, while in non-verbal communication you converse through your whole body.

NON-VERBAL MATCHING AND TRUST

Trustworthy communication comprises:

Body language – including dress, movement, facial expressions, arm gestures, eye contact, proximity, height, gender, age, and race.

Tone of voice – including whether we are soft, loud, high-pitched, quiet, rapid, gradual, hesitant, confident, pauses.

Verbal content – our words. Verbal content accounts for just 7 per cent of trustworthy communication.

When all three elements are aligned, body language, tone of voice, and words, you have a very clear, convincing message. If there is a mismatch between the three elements, the non-verbal takes precedence.

When they first meet you, people quickly decide whether or not they can trust and respect you. Trust correlates with warmth and respect correlates with competence. Ideally, you want to be perceived as both warm and competent.

The judgements we make about people align with the decisions we reach about their warmth and competence. If you are naturally a warm and trustworthy person, it makes things easier, but some people simply don't have super 'trust me' signals. These people have to work a bit harder.

This isn't about faking warmth and trustworthiness. It's about observing others, and practising those behaviours such as tone of voice and body language that signal warmth and trustworthiness.

Nevertheless, whether you are naturally warm or not, these qualities are strongly conveyed simply by a sincere approach to matching. You will be more comfortable, and so will the other person, if you match their non-verbal messages. Matching reduces the need to hold conflicting views in our head at the same time. The term for this internal conflict is **cognitive dissonance.**

Matching involves:

- Aligning all three elements of communication – body language, voice tone, and verbal content.
- Paying more attention to how you present your communication, beyond just the words themselves.
- Carefully observing and imitating the non-verbal communication of the other person.

Matching needs to be done respectfully and subtly. When you achieve this, the other person will not be conscious of what you are doing.

SUMMARY OF MATCHING SKILLS

- Watch and listen.
- Make eye contact.
- Ensure your message is congruent – keep body language, tone of voice, and words aligned.
- Match beliefs, meaning, context, worldview, and expectation.
- Be present and open.

5

IN5FLUENCING

> 'Imitation is natural to man from childhood ... he is the most imitative creature in the world, and learns at first by imitation.'
>
> **– Aristotle**

Influential communication is not just speaking. It requires technical skill, concentration, flexibility, and courage. Influential communication involves verbal communication, non-verbal communication, and listening.

Communication can be affected by a huge range of things, including our emotions, the cultural situation, the medium used to communicate, and even our location. Accurate, effective, and unambiguous communication is actually extremely hard, which is why good communication skills are considered so desirable by employers around the world.

Poor communication is the most commonly occurring problem raised in staff satisfaction surveys. This negative feedback is accurate. Despite our increasing understanding of the complexity of communication, we still communicate very poorly.

DISCOUNTING

Poor communication starts with the way problems are approached. There are four different levels to a negative approach to problems, from discounting their existence, to discounting their significance, to discounting the possibility of a solution, to discounting the possibility that *you* could solve the problem.

Discounting existence

This is mostly due to lack of good self-awareness and poor observation. In this instance, the person will be unaware of their firm's toxic culture. They will be unaware of their raised voice and gritted teeth, which means they will be unconsciously contributing to building conflict. They will fail to observe that their manager has not spoken up at the last four meetings. Such blindness always escalates, and what was a small issue becomes a black hole that sucks everyone in. Discounting the existence of problems is very poor leadership.

Discounting significance

In this instance, even if the person does notice that there are problems, they discount the significance of raising their voice and gritting their teeth, and they discount that the manger's silence is possibly important. The view is that 'we are all grown-ups here' and 'people stuff' is considered to be a distraction. Discounting the significance of problems is lazy leadership.

Discounting the possibility of change

In this instance, the person will notice the issue and believe it is significant, but discount the possibility that there is anything that could be done about the problems. The person doesn't recognise that there are options. Discounting the possibility of change is limited leadership.

Discounting personal abilities

In this instance, the person notices the issue, believes it is significant and is aware that options exist which could bring results, but they dismiss their ability to be the person who can create change and solve the problems. Discounting personal abilities shows either a lack of self-belief or a lack of relevant skills.

LEADERS COMMUNICATE VERY POORLY

Most of us still, by default, act as if communication is merely conversation. As a result, the majority of leaders believe they are excellent communicators. However, in reality, the majority of leaders discount, underestimate, and overlook how much effort is required to make every single conversation effective and influential.

We can define influence as the capacity to have an effect on the character, development, or behaviour of someone or something, or the effect itself.

Trust is an emotional skill that is essential to true influence. You need to be in tune with the hearts and minds of the people you are working with, as well as the context in which you are working. Flexibility and individual matching is the way to do this.

Trust does not need to be all or nothing. Developing a relationship with somebody often involves gauging how trustworthy that person is overall, and gaining a sense of how trustworthy they will be in particular situations.

This means that influence is about building an area of mutual trust between you and the other person with reference to the matter at hand. Look for what sustains them. Take the perspective of the other person and adapt your messages accordingly.

THE INFLUENCE DIMENSIONS TEST

The Influence Dimensions Test is your individual way to understand your unique leadership communication approach, and more importantly, how to use your style to be an influential leader with each person.

Your ID profile is unique. It is your most familiar, comfortable way of expressing yourself. Study the descriptions in the following pages and make an estimate of your own unique ID profile. Of the four styles and six dimensions consider which descriptions best fit your most common ways of communicating. This will be a fairly accurate measure of your patterns.

Write down your ID profile and set it out in the same way as the ID sample shown in this link: http://www.mcpheeandrewartha.com.au/corporate-consultancy/products-publications/publications/influence-dimensions-comm-report/

Keep and use this sample profile as a template for building your own ID profile. After reading the descriptions in the following paragraphs, write down your ID style and dimensions.

Your ID profile makes your matched communication conscious. Your ID pattern reveals how you communicate most of the time. For example, I am very **Rapid,** and say and do things quickly and reactively most of the time if I am not consciously matching the other person. Therefore, I also have rapid expectations of others. However, I am very **Gradual** when buying a car or a house.

As a leader you will already be unconsciously matching others, so you will find you are often using one of the four styles and many of the six dimensions in your communication with others.

Your ID profile is a record of the most effective ways of communicating you have deliberately built up and reinforced over the years. It is how you naturally communicate without thinking about it.

To be influential, you need to have excellent self-awareness of your ID behaviours all the time, and also to be attuned to the other person's ID patterns, so you can match them.

Your ID will help you have more impactful conversations by:

- Understanding how your profile shapes the way you converse.
- Understanding how your profile shapes the way the other person will converse.
- Using knowledge of how your profile shapes the way the other person will converse to reframe the way you converse.

Once you study your profile you will be well-equipped to make an accurate estimate of the critical parts of the other person's ID profile in relationship to your own, and use it to shape the way you say your words.

The ID reveals the meaning and non-verbal influence governing how your words are conveyed. In COVID screen times, this means you can match what the words mean.

Things to note about your profile

1. No set of dimensions represents the best way to lead. We are all different types of leaders. The best leadership occurs when we match our communication to the other person.

2. Your ID profile is only casually connected to your personality. With effort you can change your ID. It requires therapy to change your personality.

3. Your ID profile is not a fixed label. You will display some characteristics from the other end of the continuum many times. Leaders need to be flexible in their communication, and tend to match others unconsciously. As a result, we will sometimes operate outside our profile.

4. When you are stressed or under pressure or threatened, you will always revert to your ID profile pattern.

There are two interrelated parts to your ID profile – your **Influence Style,** and your **Six Communication Dimensions.**

THE FOUR INFLUENCE STYLES

How to identify and match other people's Influence Style.

Your profile will show the way you unconsciously approach and conduct your conversations. You will have considered *what* you want to say, but much more significantly, this will assist you in *how* you will say it. It helps in many of the matching elements we discussed above, namely, context, worldview, meaning, and expectation.

If your profile is similar to the other person's, the conversation will proceed reasonably well without much thought required.

If you have different profiles, you are less likely to feel familiar, and less likely to be easily trusted. You will be more effective in conducting the conversation if you modify your presentation so that it matches more closely the other person's way of understanding.

Look at the communication style on your ID profile. Are you identified as an Analyser, a Planner, a Creator, a Developer, or some combination of two of these?

As you will see from the sample report, Planners and Analysers are similar in overall approach, and Creators and Developers are alike. The former have more difficulty matching with the latter, and vice versa.

Unless you have seen the other person's ID profile, you will need to evaluate their communication style and dimensions based on your observation of them. You don't need years of practise to do this. With simple observation you can make very accurate assessments quite quickly.

IF YOU ARE AN ANALYSER

You are likely to approach leadership as a matter of rules and principle. You work from a bedrock of correctness.

You are methodical and diligent, and not in a big rush. There is a right way and a wrong way of doing things. If a core rule has been broken, it needs to be corrected. The rule needs to be clarified and followed. You work carefully towards the best result in a thorough and systematic way. You don't like mistakes. There is less emotional display, and you may appear off-putting. You are often sceptical, and like to be well-prepared. You are less of a 'people' communicator and more of a 'problem-solving' communicator.

This is the expectation you bring to the discussion. It will tend to exert an influence on how you lead. Consider your Analyser 'tells' and how these might impact on your conversation.

EXAMPLE – AN ANALYSER SPEAKING ABOUT A CREATOR MANAGER

'I disciplined him fairly and properly. The compliance rules are posted in the manual and he knows what they are. He didn't follow them, and out of spite probably. He dared to argue that rules are not the be all and end all. Really! The place would descend to chaos without rules. Docking him a day's pay for not filing the report in the right place will send a message to the others too.'

IF YOU ARE A PLANNER

As a leader, you want to organise the situation and map out the beginning, the middle, and the end of the matter. You prefer to schedule the conversation and plan out each of the stages, so you don't waste time.

You want to run things and get the matter completed. You tend to be a little direct and candid. Planners focus on the conversation and don't worry so much about the relationship after the discussion. You lean towards telling and not asking.

This is the expectation you bring to the discussion. It will tend to exert an influence on the other person, regardless of their style. Consider your Planner 'tells' and how these might impact on your conversation.

EXAMPLE – A MEETING GONE WRONG, FROM A PLANNER'S PERSPECTIVE, EXAMPLE – AN

ANALYSER SPEAKING ABOUT A CREATOR MANAGER

Thomas sat silently seething. It was ten minutes past the hour. The Directors' meeting should have started on time. Where were his two co-directors? He looked at his watch for the hundredth time. He looked at the business folders laid out in front of each director's chair, notepaper alongside, pencil at the top, agenda on the first page, last month's minutes. All properly prepared.

Where were they?

Monica and Charles burst into the room laughing.

Charles throws his sandwich on top of the carefully aligned business folder in front of his chair and takes a swig from his bottle of cola. 'Hi Tommy', he says cheerfully.

'Charles,' Thomas gives a tight nod of the head. 'Shall we start? You are late, both of you.'

'Oops,' Monica giggles.

'OK, let's proceed. There is a chart projection in the appendix that is relevant for the first agenda item. If you will both turn to that now.'

'Oh, do we have to do this matter? It never seems to go away,' exclaims Monica. 'I'd rather focus on the new office. Yes, let's talk about the design for that.'

'It is Item Five on the agenda.'

'Yes, but we always seem to be working on this bloody projection. I'm so sick of it', Charles cuts in.

'That's because you two never settle long enough to make a decision about it!' retorts Thomas.

And so the meeting continues. Sometimes they made progress, but often they become sidetracked with frustration and exasperation.

This is an example of poor matching between a Planner (Thomas) and his partners, a Creator (Monica), and a Developer (Charles).

In general, Thomas considers himself very orderly and focused. He likes to get things done properly, in the correct sequence, and in detail. The others see him as fussy and obsessive. He irritates them because he is so precise and tunnel-visioned. In their view, he invites being teased. He is quick, but only when he knows exactly where he is going. New, unexpected directions with no boundaries and no agreed timelines are seen as distractions. Thomas might agree that Charles and Monica's impulsive sidetracks are often brilliant, but the spontaneity of their presentations without any context really throw him off-balance and disturbs him. On top of which, they are continuously cracking jokes, but it feels as though they are laughing at him, not with him.

Thomas and his co-directors would benefit from arranging for one in every three meetings to be unplanned, with no agenda, no focus, and a loose timescale. If necessary, they could invite an outside facilitator to help keep things open and unconstrained. Monica and Charles could coach Thomas in allowing himself to use more imagination in these free-flowing meetings.

Equally, Thomas could coach Monica and Charles to focus more fully on *all* the items on the agenda during the two structured meetings, not just those they consider to be of value. They could be encouraged to be punctual and to let Thomas take the lead in these more structured meetings, as he fulfils this role so well.

IF YOU ARE A CREATOR

As a leader, you are quite content stepping into the unknown, responding spontaneously by saying what you think and feel, without being too concerned about where the conversation might go. You speak your thoughts.

Creators tend to be dramatic and all over the place in conversation, so it can be hard to understand precisely where the focus lies. You may interrupt and go off on tangents, using a range of voice tones and gestures to support your changing message.

This is the expectation you bring to the discussion which will tend to exert an influence on the other person, regardless of their style. Consider your Creator 'tells' and how these might impact on your conversation.

EXAMPLE – CREATIVE SPIRIT

'It's utterly incredible! It's unbelievable! The best ever!' an exhausted Geoff exclaims.

'Oh this is fun. We get paid for this?' Jianling adds.

'It is a great concept isn't it?' Trevor chips in. 'It will really sell well.'

The room was a mess. Empty food containers, leftover drinks, papers, samples, and shoes scattered everywhere. The three had been working on a new marketing campaign for their pharmaceutical company's latest product, which had just been approved by the government.

They had been away at a retreat resort for the last three days. They had worked each day till they dropped, with hundreds of ideas developed and tons of energy to do the work. There had been fights and screaming matches, there had been hugs and laughter—lots of laughter. Some of the ideas had been ridiculous. They had brainstormed one concept after another, piling up ideas, some of which would never see the light of day.

It had been a three-day, free-flowing, emotional roller-coaster ride. There were no goals, no parameters, and no rules. Anything and everything had been up for grabs, even the name of the product!

Tired but excited they had dinner and retired.

The next day they returned to the city and left their marketing plan with Wayne, the national sales manager.

Wayne was an Analyser. He had come to respect the company's marketing people over the last few years. He looked through the report, ignoring the spelling errors and incorrect grammar, and overlooking the layout and presentation. He also stopped himself reacting to the totally unacceptable costs of some aspects of their plan, preferring to concentrate on the essence of their ideas.

As an Analyser, Wayne knew that all the details could be built up later, provided the core concept worked. The marketing team had an excellent process. They went off alone and came up with ideas that were better than anything anyone else in the company could achieve. They did this in ways that would drive anyone else mad, but where was the problem? These ideas just needed an analytical frame to turn them into an affordable campaign. The order and detail imposed at the end combined with their fresh, spontaneous creativity to make for an excellent campaign.

IF YOU ARE A DEVELOPER

The context for you as a leader starts with the other person's feelings and position. Before the conversation even begins you are already down the path of not wanting to be mistaken and cause offence. You like friendly, interactive conversations. You want to get what you want by being nice and reasonable.

You may build great rapport without actually accomplishing anything. You may be tempted to make concessions to appease others, and hope they will reciprocate.

Of the four approaches, Developers are the most uncomfortable with clearly addressing topics that may possibly upset others.

This is the expectation you bring to the discussion which will tend to exert an influence on the other person, regardless of their style. Consider your Developer 'tells' and how these might impact on your conversation.

EXAMPLE – DEVELOPING STRATEGIES

Webster's hardware store was in crisis. The new supermarket hardware chains had eroded their customer base, and their profits. The five staff worked long hours, seven days a week, just to try and keep their heads above water. The salaries were killing them, as were the excessive hours. Now they were fighting—there was conflict in a team whose members had always got on well with each other.

The team comprised a nice mixture of Influence styles, with two Analysers who ran the place and did the books, a Creator who was the best salesperson, a Planner who set up new stock and arranged the displays, and a Developer who charmed the zoning authorities and customers alike.

It fell to the Developer to help them find their way out of the conflict and the challenges the business was facing. She worked tirelessly with the reality presented to her of the declining trade. She had the perseverance and lateral ideas to hang in there, and also to develop new possibilities. She side-tracked her friends when they were getting too heated by using connections to their supportive history. She gradually developed enthusiasm in the team for the company to specialise by offering skilled, tailored advice on handyman needs. She generated respect and belief in her colleagues, the authorities, and the store's customers. She believed in the long term. She held them together. She identified their differences and reminded them all of why those differences were so valuable. She reshaped them using their own characteristics.

LEADERSHIP STYLES SUMMARY

A gentle caricature of each of these styles may illustrate each of them in a different light.

Analysers want to do the right thing the right way. They don't mind, or even notice, if people are upset or bothered. They must complete the task no matter what.

Planners map out an agenda or a project outline, with timelines and KPIs. They encourage people to get on board, and expect them to 'colour inside the lines'.

Creators go in full tilt. They have fun, changing topics and goals in a heartbeat. They want people to be engaged, but don't notice if they aren't. Their focus is not on how to achieve the goal – their focus is on how shiny and bright they can make it look.

Developers really hate discord and will do anything to ensure everybody gets on. They don't like start-ups, but enjoy pulling things together and maintaining the business over the long haul. They would rather miss the goal than see the team upset.

IF YOU ARE AN ANALYSER OR PLANNER...

If the person you are engaging with appears to be well-organised, fairly formal, and talks as though things need to follow rules and a plan, they are likely to also be a Planner or Analyser. Therefore, communicate as you normally would.

However, if they seem unprepared, disorganised, dramatic, sociable, amiable, interested in people getting on, and have poor time-management skills, then they are likely to be a Developer or Creator.

To be more successful communicating with them try these matching tips:

(a) Be prepared to be caught off guard.

(b) Be a little more flexible and open in the way you present the matter to them.

(c) Reveal some of your own feelings or concerns.

(d) Smile.

(e) Show that concern for others is also important to you.

(f) Listen to, and acknowledge, their divergent views.

(g) Let the session wander a bit.

(h) Consider there may be other ways to resolve the issue.

(i) Reconsider your assumptions about them.

IF YOU ARE A DEVELOPER OR CREATOR...

If the other person appears energetic, flexible, concerned about others, open, and flexible, they are likely to be a Developer or Creator. Therefore, communicate as you normally would.

However, if they seem serious, off-putting, strict, inflexible, focused on rules or procedures, overly factual, and very organised, then they are likely to be a Planner or Analyser.

To be more successful communicating with them try these matching tips:

(a) Accept this is their way of approaching things.

(b) Look serious.

(c) Try to follow their steps until you can share your thoughts.

(d) Minimise friendly non-matched chit chat.

(e) Reconsider your assumptions about them.

(f) Try to consolidate your ideas into general themes.

(g) Give evidence to support the importance of the 'people stuff'.

EXERCISE – INFLUENCE STYLES

Take a moment to reflect on your Influence style and those of some of your colleagues and clients.

My Influence style is

....

....

In my view, the Influence styles of my colleagues and clients are:

Person One (name and style)

....

....

Person Two (name and style)

....

....

Person Three (name and style)

....

....

Person Four (name and style)

....

....

Person Five (name and style)

....

....

Person Six (name and style)

....

....

Person Seven (name and style)

....

....

Person Eight (name and style)

....

....

EXERCISE – EFFECTIVELY USING ID PROFILES

Reflecting on your past interactions with each of these people, does this ID frame offer you any thoughts about being more effective next time?

If so, list your thoughts here

....
....
....
....
....
....
....
....
....
....
....
....

We are all unique, and so matching is an ongoing process of continuous observation and adjustment. When you feel you are not connecting well, change something, anything, to better match what you are observing in the other person.

Matching the other person's Influence Style, in combination with matching their ID Dimensions, increases effective influence and trust.

Trust can be rebuilt, even when it may have been seriously damaged. Trust, despite what you may have been told, is not built in years and destroyed in seconds.

NEUROSCIENCE OF THE INFLUENCE DIMENSIONS

Words, the 7 per cent of communication that conveys verbal information, also reveal a non-verbal element in their method of presentation. Your ID profile captures that non-verbal element.

The type of words you use are alerts to your intentions and expectations, revealing the meaning behind your words. Understanding this and matching your counterpart enables you to become more trusted and, therefore, more influential.

The ID identifies your specific pattern of word use across six universal dimensions. Knowing your patterns helps you match the other person's patterns fairly simply. It doesn't take a lot to make a match. It's like speaking a few words of the language in another country – you don't need to be fluent to receive positive recognition.

Use the guide below to enhance your matching fluency. The more Dimensions you are able to match, the stronger your trust, familiarity, and influence.

Mismatching, whether it is unconscious or deliberate, feels uncomfortable, like you have missed the mark somehow. It is disjunctive, and the conversation will hesitate, change track, or break down completely.

THE SIX ID DIMENSIONS

On the sample ID template, each Dimension is shown as a continuum. For example, the Timing Dimension shows a line from Gradual on the left to Rapid on the right. If you are dead centre that means you are balanced on that particular Dimension, and match either side equally easily.

1. The Timing Dimension: Rapid/Gradual Processors

In our communication with others we vary in the speed of our delivery, the timing of our messages, our sense of urgency, and the time we take to process information.

When the timing is just right for both parties, the message is conveyed and received as intended.

When the pace is too fast the receiver feels rushed and pressured, and responds to this influencing factor, often misreading the message or not responding at the optimal level.

If the timing is too slow the responder can discount the significance of the communication or become irritated by the slowness of delivery and question the credibility of the person communicating.

Mastering timing means successfully matching your presentation to the behaviours of the people you are interacting with.

Rapid processor

Let's do it now – all of it.

We must move quickly to pick up this opportunity.

Expression: *A stitch in time saves nine*

Rapid processors like to receive all the information quickly and are frustrated by delays, hesitations in speech, and changes to decisions.

They tend to rush ahead without taking in significant peripheral detail or other possible options. They tend to be impatient with people who present information slowly and who need time to deliberate, often inaccurately labelling them as unintelligent, obstructive, and uncooperative, or uncommitted to achieving goals.

Rapids are like city slickers – fast-paced and hectic.

As leaders, Rapid processors do well with major tasks that have tight deadlines and require immediate action, and where many things need to be coordinated simultaneously. They tend to get bored with slow-moving tasks with little risk or challenge, seeing them as tedious and mundane.

Rapid processors never miss an opportunity, but they often rush headlong into mistakes and do not take advantage of new information that may have become available since they made their original decision.

Rapids tend to use phrases like 'Hurry up', 'Come on', 'Quickly', 'Let's do it now', 'Why wait?', 'There's no time', 'Move it', 'How much longer?', and 'Are we there yet?'

Gradual processor

Let's take it slowly and carefully.

We really must take time to consider this fully.

Expression: *More haste less speed*

Gradual processors tend to be overwhelmed if too much data is presented too quickly, or if they are pressured to make decisions before they have enough time to deliberate.

They like to take in each element and digest it thoroughly before absorbing the next. As leaders, they tend to take things as they come. They often have an accepting optimistic attitude to change, expecting it will all work out in the end. Graduals are like country folk – everything is slow and easy.

Gradual processors like small, well-defined, and narrowly-focused tasks, or major projects with long time-frames so they can establish project milestones and complete the work in a considered manner.

They tend to be less competent in high-pressure, high change situations. Gradual processors rarely make impulsive mistakes, but they can miss out on golden opportunities.

Common phrases used by graduals are 'Now just a minute', 'There's no hurry', 'Where's the fire?', 'Take it easy', 'Slow down', 'We're nearly there', 'Won't be a minute', and 'Phew! It happened so quickly'.

Timing differences

Rapid and Gradual are two different communication styles. They are two sides of the timing continuum. Our personality does contribute a little to our communication patterns, yet Rapid and Gradual are **not** personality types. They are *behaviours* that can change and develop with practise.

The ways we have of relating to the world are shaped in part by whether we are Rapid or Gradual. Rapids tend to see things as faster than they actually are. Graduals tend to see things as slower and more manageable than they might really be.

Of course, most of us have some behaviours from both the Gradual and the Rapid ends of the seesaw. Rarely are any of us purely Rapid with no Gradual elements at all, or exclusively Gradual without any dashes of Rapid.

Matching

Rapids match and are comfortable with each other, just as Graduals match and are comfortable with each other. They are in tune at a subliminal level.

Rapid processors are well-matched with other rapid processors, but together they can speedily fly off on a tangent to the rest of the group. They may find Gradual processors too slow to deal with respectfully. To communicate more effectively with their Gradual processor colleagues, Rapids could break up their information into smaller, more manageable bits, and wait to get confirmation before going on.

Rapid processors need to appreciate the more Gradual style of others if they are to be successful.

Gradual processors match well with other gradual processors and discuss matters in a calm and methodical manner.

Graduals can match better with Rapids if they speak a little more quickly and have fewer pauses between words and sentences. Using words such as fast, quickly, and short-term, and appreciating the energy level of the Rapid can help Graduals in their communication, as can throwing in a few quick gesticulations.

Mismatching

Rapid processors and Gradual processors are mismatched and often uncomfortable with each other. Such mismatching is the source of prejudice or bias. It is possible for Rapids to dismiss Graduals as being too uninterested or even uncommitted. Certainly, they stretch the patience of their Rapid colleagues. Gradual people may feel that a Rapid person is too superficial and doesn't give enough thought to things. They often see them as error prone.

For these reasons, Rapid processors and Gradual processors tend to have a mild distrust of each other's ability in dealing with problems, projects, or group activities. At worst, this can create irritation that may eventually lead to subversion of the group's effectiveness.

EXERCISE – RAPID/GRADUAL INTERACTIONS

Make some notes regarding important Rapid/Gradual interactions that you have experienced as a leader.

Rapid/Gradual interactions I have experienced include

_____

2. The Emphasis Dimension: Exaggerators And Understaters

The way we tend to emphasise things contributes significantly to the level of importance others place on those things. With too little emphasis something may be viewed as trivial or not very important. Too much emphasis on something may convey implausibility or overreaction.

Exaggerators

Wow! This is unbelievably effective. I'm totally committed to this process.

Expression: *You should have seen the one that got away*

Exaggerators tend to over-emphasise the importance of things and blow things out of proportion. They make mountains out of molehills. They have an enthusiasm, an energy, and a noticeable reaction to events. When things are good they are visibly excited and often demonstrative. When things are bad they react quite strongly and negatively.

They are expansive, energetic, and want to make a big impact. They are creative with the truth and often present things as extremes. They react to life. They find it hard to use qualifiers. For exaggerators things are all or nothing.

Exaggerators tend to use words like incredible, disaster, impossible, absolutely, definitely, completely, no, yes, rubbish, never, and always.

Understaters

Yes, this is fairly useful. This process has some merit.

Expression: *Everything in moderation*

Understaters play things down. They tend to be low-key. It is often hard to tell how things affect them. They provide little body language and minimal voice inflection. They are quiet and may appear to be shy in their overall presentation.

Understaters don't get overly exuberant about good news and they don't get overly reactive about bad news. They tend to be very good poker players, and are quite likely to be on an even keel about most things. They adapt to life.

Common words used by Understaters include perhaps, maybe, a little, some, sometimes, occasionally, sort of, moderately, possibly.

Matching

Being an Exaggerator or an Understater is not linked to accomplishment. Exaggerators can be very flamboyant and achieve very little, and Understaters can be very low-key and quite modest in their presentation, and yet achieve significant things.

Exaggerators tend to see other Exaggerators as 'good', whereas Understaters are considered to be not quite as good. Similarly, Understaters unconsciously prefer Understaters, and don't feel so comfortable with Exaggerators. In both cases, what is familiar is good, and what is unfamiliar is uncomfortable.

Exaggerators and Exaggerators match with each other. Understaters and Understaters match with each other. They are in tune at a subliminal level. It is literally unconscious understanding.

Exaggerators naturally understand and accept exaggeration in each other. They don't take it too seriously. They share a sense of drama and passion about things. Two Exaggerators though, can be quite hysterical if there is a fire! Understaters also accept each other. They don't equate the low-key presentation with a lack of commitment or energy. They delve into things in the same manner.

Mismatching

Exaggerators and Understaters are mismatched and may be uncomfortable with each other.

It is possible for exaggerators to dismiss the ideas of Understaters and not take them very seriously. In the eyes of Exaggerators, Understaters don't seem really committed or involved.

Understaters may perceive exaggerators as dismissive of their ideas and difficult to persuade. They seem like hustlers. They are pushy, and sometimes, can be viewed as liars. To an Understater, an Exaggerator often seems phony and insincere. Ironically, insincerity is often a view shared by both sides – Exaggerators are seen as insincere by Understaters because they blow things up out of all proportion. Understaters are seen as insincere by Exaggerators because they tend not to show energy and commitment. Such mismatching is the source of prejudice. In terms of poor communication it is the case that:

• Understaters can overlook Exaggerators, due to perceiving them as being too over the top.

• Exaggerators can overlook Understaters, due to perceiving them as being too quiet or gentle.

Exaggerators often tend to regard Understaters as boring, uninteresting, not committed, unenthusiastic or low-key. On the other hand, Understaters often regard

Exaggerators as over-reactors, hustlers, show-offs, liars, insincere, not genuine, and too over the top.

Understaters feel overpowered and excessively pressured by Exaggerators. Exaggerators feel unmoved and unmotivated by Understaters.

Wherever there is a mismatch in these two elements, there is automatically a different sense of meaning, and a different emphasis attached to the same subject. As a result of this, the likelihood for misunderstanding is very strong.

Even where there is no difference between the two people in terms of intent and values, they can still feel as though they don't really agree with each other.

It is important to remember that these behaviours of 'Exaggerator' and 'Understater' are communication styles, not personality types. Exaggerators may be nice or nasty. Understaters can be good or bad. There is nothing positive or negative about being one or the other. The goal though, is to maximise our understanding of the other person's communication style by matching it!

Exaggerators are not necessarily extroverts, and Understaters are not always introverts. An extrovert (showy, life of the party, larger than life) can understate in their communication. All their words are correct and factual. There is no lying or hyperbole.

Similarly an introvert (shy, quiet, withdrawn, low-key) can exaggerate. Examples of this would be, 'I never seem to get things right', 'I am always hopeless at planning' and so on. Often there is a match between personality and ID, but not always.

EXERCISE – EXAGGERATOR/UNDERSTATER INTERACTIONS

Make some notes regarding important Exaggerator/Understater interactions that you have had as a leader.

Important Exaggerator/Understater interactions I have had include

....
....
....
....
....
....
....
....
....
....
....
....
....
....
....
....

3. The Thinking Dimension: Linear And Lateral Thinkers

We all store, analyse, and communicate information in two distinct ways. Our analytical process can either be linear (sequential, ordered, and planned) or lateral (random, creative, and associative). These two kinds of analytical processes mix like oil and water, and the people at opposite ends of the scale often have difficulties in communicating with each other and working together.

Linear thinkers

Let's approach this one step at a time. I can see where we need to go from here.

Expression: *A place for everything, and everything in its place*

Linear thinkers are focused, ordered, sequential and uni-directional in their thought processes.

The linear thinker tends to take things one step at a time, in a chronological order or a predetermined fashion. Linear thinkers are also orderly in the way they approach tasks. They tend to study street directories and follow them in a systematic manner. They like methodical tasks with set routines, rules, and well-defined guidelines. Linear thinkers tend to run a meeting by the established rules, and find it difficult to be flexible with changes to the agenda or set procedures. They are less comfortable with ambiguous guidelines, tasks, and circumstances.

Linear thinkers are predictable and constitutional. They believe in antecedents, constitutions, rules, procedures, and the past. They rely on precedents and a solid foundation for starting any communication. They like to set the stage, prepare the agenda, and know where they stand before commencing. They are formal and constrained, logical and efficient. They follow patterns and are reliable in debating issues.

Linear folks often use phrases like: 'First we do this, next we do that', 'Let's put things in order', 'The agenda is...', 'That's not in the rules', 'Here's the plan', 'The correct procedure is...', 'Meetings should start on time', 'There's a time and place for things'.

Lateral thinkers

There are so many ways we can approach this.

Forget about Step One, let's go on to Step Four and consider that suggestion again.

Expression: *There's more than one way to skin a cat*

Lateral thinkers enjoy working in a broad context when making decisions, planning actions, or solving problems. They move from one aspect of the problem to another with no discernible connection or linkage to matters previously discussed. They initiate ideas, often without others understanding the basis for their leap of thought. As leaders they are innovative and creative in their thought processes, and often save groups from being bogged down in set paradigms or fixed opinions.

They relate well when they are able to ask questions and formulate ideas based on what can often appear to be random or unpredictable processes. They tend to have variable routines, and may have so much flexibility that it is difficult to pin them down to definite arrangements. Lateral people often don't directly answer the question they are asked, if at all. They often answer a question with a question.

Lateral thinkers invent new rules, ignore old ones, go off on tangents, and are innovative about everything. The slogan, 'Today is the first day of the rest of your life' was coined by a Lateral. They start out in left field, from nowhere, heading in the wrong direction, changing ideas mid-sentence. Laterals are informal and flexible, creative and challenging. They can pronounce on a belief one day, and yet genuinely support the opposite view on the next.

They often use phrases like: 'On the one hand ... but on the other hand', 'Where did I put my glasses?', 'Let's do this – no, on second thoughts, let's do that', 'Let's re-examine our whole premise', 'Do it anyway', 'What rules?', and 'Ask for it anyway, even if it isn't on the menu'.

Matching

Linear thinkers match with other Linears. They are familiar, recognisable, and comfortable to one another, and are therefore easily understood.

Because they are matched, two or more Linears can manage a discussion very efficiently and effectively. Time is managed perfectly, all agenda items are addressed, and all outcomes are achieved. They can also be boring and predictable. The outcomes may be efficient, but they are rarely exciting, breathtaking, or fun. Such an encounter may seem superficial and predictable to a Lateral.

Lateral people are naturally compatible with their Lateral colleagues and friends. Their compatibility ensures an exciting energetic meeting that roams all over the place. Time is shredded, not managed. Past decisions are revisited and reworked. Some meetings produce no outcomes at all, while others create some outstandingly awe-inspiring ideas. It sometimes looks like a mess to a Linear person.

Mismatching

Linear thinkers and Lateral thinkers do not match with each other.

Without trust, they can be amused, irritated, confused, dismissive, or judgemental of one another. Even with respect and trust, they can still be amused, irritated, confused, dismissive, and judgemental with each other!

Linear people can sometimes perceive Lateral thinkers as scatterbrained, disorganised, and illogical. They feel that Lateral people are unable to keep on track, and if allowed to proceed unchecked, that Laterals would go down all sorts of sidetracks and prevent the group from achieving its goals efficiently.

Lateral thinkers may perceive Linear people as rigid, uncreative, and boring. They feel that Linears are obsessed with rules and protocol. They are seen as narrow-minded people who miss out on variety and alternatives.

EXERCISE – LINEAR/LATERAL INTERACTIONS

Make some notes regarding important Linear/Lateral interactions that you have had as a leader.

Important Linear/Lateral interactions I have had as a leader include

---

4. The Focus Dimension: Detailer And Conceptualiser

The fourth dimension of influence is that of focus. Most situations involve a need to be familiar with both the detail and conceptual framework of whatever is being discussed. However, we vary in the focus we bring to tasks. At one end of the scale we have Detailers, and at the other end, Conceptualisers.

To communicate successfully with a Detailer about an exciting concept you need to be prescriptive and exact in your presentation. To communicate successfully with a Conceptualiser you need to talk about the big picture—the context, or in some cases the goals and outcomes to be achieved, or even the background or theoretical framework for the discussion, *before* launching into the details.

Detailers need a build-up to a concept, through the provision of specific points, usually linked to something they already understand. To gain the attention and support of a Conceptualiser, you need to start with the desired end and then fill in the details necessary for attainment of the goal.

Detailers

Let me see all the details.

There are some points to address before we make the decision.

Expression: *Cross the Ts and dot the Is*

Detailers examine each specific element that is essential to achieving a task. They may make lists of the facts or issues about a project before making a decision about anything. They may resent being diverted from this process and will refuse to look at the bottom line or the policy, concept, or outcome under consideration without first gathering what they perceive to be all of the relevant information.

Detailers excel at tasks where accuracy is essential to the achievement of the goal. Detailers are more confident once a project has been scoped and clear information is available about the background, the expected end results, a time frame, and resource allocation. At their worst, detailers often can't see the forest for the trees and become inefficient or unable to make decisions, as new information constantly comes to hand.

Favourite words include precisely, in point of fact, actually, look here, exactly, and finite.

Conceptualisers

What's the bottom line?

Here's my vision for the future...

Expression: *I have a dream.*

Those concerned with the overall concept need to have the purpose and context of the matter addressed before they can be comfortably engaged in the task. Details may seem irrelevant to them and better left to others, or they are happy to pick up the details after establishing the bottom line.

Conceptualisers tend to make good motivators and marketers. They are the people with vision and goal orientation. They are initially concerned about the value of the project or task, and until they are satisfied that the basic goal can be achieved and is worth achieving, their involvement is tentative. Occasionally, in a meeting about a task, they may overlook an important detail or be slow to move to action because the concepts are so enjoyable to discuss.

Words often used by Conceptualisers are imagine, big picture, bottom line, outside the square, we can do it, vision, and the future.

Matching

Detailers find other detailers familiar and easy to understand. They have the same focus and interests. They combine well for audits, editing, and all conversations covering the finer points of an idea or project.

Conceptualisers really enjoy envisioning the future with other 'big picture' people. Together they dream or connect on the core issues of any matter.

Mismatching

Detailers and Conceptualisers do not match well with each other. Detailers find it hard to grasp the subject matter with a concept person, as their pie-in-the-sky pictures seem so unrealistic and fantasy-like.

Conceptualisers, on the other hand, are often irritated by the apparent negativity and demotivating responses of the Detailer, who seems to ask lots of picky, trivial, troublesome questions. Detailers are often overlooked by conceptualisers because they are seen as petty nit-pickers who can't see the forest for the trees. Conceptualisers are often overlooked by detailers because they are impractical dreamers who can't see the trees for the forest.

EXERCISE –
DETAILER/CONCEPTUALISER
INTERACTIONS

Make some notes regarding important Detailer/Conceptualiser interactions you have had as a leader.

Important Detailer/Conceptualiser interactions I have had as a leader include

....
....
....
....
....
....
....
....
....
....
....
....
....
....
....
....
....
....
....
....
....

5. The Evaluation Dimension: Self-Evaluator/Other-Evaluator

Our way of evaluating things affects our receptiveness to feedback and new ideas. At one end of the scale we have self-evaluators, who tend to be inward looking and take responsibility for all outcomes. This adds a self-questioning flavour to all their interactions. At the other end we have other-evaluators, who focus externally and therefore have the opposite view of who is responsible for outcomes. They look at the context or others who can be held responsible when things go wrong.

Self-evaluators

I got that wrong.

I'm sorry—I should have anticipated your question.

Expression: *It's all my fault.*

When things go wrong, self-evaluators tend to assess their contribution and their need to change, in a critical or evaluative manner. They tend, at least initially, to overlook the role of others' contributions and behaviour when assessing what has happened. They often take too much responsibility for delegated tasks. In team situations it is unhelpful to disagree with their initial reaction, which is usually to take an unfair share of the blame when things go wrong. By matching their assessment and initially agreeing, a good leader can enable them to shift focus from their own contribution to look at others' roles.

Self-evaluating people may use phrases like: 'It's all my fault', 'I'm to blame', 'I'm responsible', 'I'm sorry', 'Excuse me', 'I hope I'm not in your way', 'Forgive me', 'I didn't mean to', 'There I go again', 'Oops', 'I', 'Me', 'My', 'If only...', 'Please', 'My fault', 'Should', and 'Why didn't I?'

Other-evaluators

That's wrong!

You should have briefed me better.

Expression: *Why don't they just fix it?*

Other-evaluators tend to evaluate the contribution of others and assess or hold others responsible for negative outcomes before evaluating their own input and responsibility. With delegated tasks they tend to be overly concerned about comparing their areas of responsibility with what others are responsible for and can be unreasonably concerned about the performance of others, instead of concentrating on their own outcomes. They may be inclined to shift responsibility on to others.

Commonly used phrases are: 'It was impossible to work in that room', 'Now I've got you', 'That's stupid', 'What's the use?', 'You just can't get good help these days', 'What would they know?', and 'Let me do it'.

Matching

In this pattern, Other-evaluators are paradoxically matched with self-evaluators because they relate well to the other person's need to discuss their performance problems. Other-evaluators can do excellent compliance and accountability work together, and they can get on well if they are discussing the stupidity of a third party. Two Self-evaluators can be well-matched, although their conversation can be gossipy or a 'pity party'.

Mismatching

Other-evaluators mismatch with both Self-evaluators and Other-evaluators when they are not using their objectivity check. When they intend to argue rather than resolve, then they are mismatching.

Self-evaluators tend to mismatch when not being assertive with an Other-evaluator, or when out-doing another Self-evaluator on a 'poor me' routine.

Evaluation is another dimension where people can get excited, as they feel a personality sensitivity instead of a communication understanding. Being Self-evaluating is about how you communicate, not what your personality is. Being Other-evaluating is about how you give feedback and assess, not what your personality is.

Here are some contrasting examples:

Healthy personalities

Self-evaluator: great self-awareness and self-development, always willing to look at what they can change about themselves.

Other-evaluator: excellent reality grounding, valued constructive feedback, evidence-based.

Less healthy personalities

Self-evaluator: self-deprecating, miserable.

Other-evaluator: bullying, always blames others.

EXERCISE – SELF-EVALUATOR/OTHER-EVALUATOR INTERACTIONS

Make some notes regarding important Self-evaluator/Other-evaluator interactions you have had as a leader.

Important Self-evaluator/Other-evaluator interactions I have had as a leader include

....
....
....
....
....
....
....
....
....
....
....
....
....
....
....
....
....
....
....

6. The Relationship Dimension: Initiator/Responder

The nature of the reactive relationship between people impacts on the way we communicate with them. When the relationship is in balance (matched), this contributes to effective outcomes. However, when the relationship is in conflict (mismatched), the misunderstanding between the two people gets in the way of effective outcomes.

The relationship pattern refers to how often and in what manner we initiate things in our relationships with others, and how often we tend to respond to the initiatives of others. At one extreme we have people we'll call initiators, and at the other end responders.

Initiators

Follow me.

Let me show you. We can meet to plan what you do next.

Expression: *Here's the plan.*

Initiators like introducing new concepts and tend to take the lead in most communication. They take the lead with ideas presented by others and take over the focus of the conversation. They tend to produce ideas and to assume the dominant position quickly.

Initiators tend to be very good in a team leadership role, but are inclined to be directive. They expect a response to their ideas and automatically tend to give directions to others. They can easily lead a meeting and they start off well with tasks, but may have difficulty finishing them. They are often seen as too pushy in situations where they are required to be more passive, such as during interviews where they have to respond and are not able to control the flow of ideas.

Phrases most often used by Initiators are: 'Listen here', 'Look here', 'Here's the plan', 'Let me show you', and 'Do this'.

Responders

I'm right behind you.

Let me get back to you on that.

Expression: *What's the plan?*

Responders like other people to take the lead. They prefer to understand the setting, the background, and the nature of the circumstances before committing themselves. They prefer to respond to others' initiatives and follow their lead. They like to have tasks clearly spelled out.

Responders are good team players and excellent people for second-in-command or supportive roles. They can be excellent leaders where democratic or participative leadership is required. They are usually matched well with Initiators, but can be less effective when communicating with other Responders. One obstacle for Responders is the fear of making a mistake.

Favourite phrases include: 'That's good', 'Great idea', 'When do you want it?', 'Are we there yet?', 'Could I suggest...?', and 'Let me help'.

Matching

The well-matched relationship is between an Initiator and a Responder. In relationships at home and at work the best complementary connection is between these opposites. The effective roles in the relationship dimension are: giver/taker, one up/one down, leader/follower. This does not mean that two Initiators cannot form an effective or compatible relationship with each other. It just requires a little more effort in give and take, a little more understanding. But they are likely to clash often.

Mismatching

An Initiator is mismatched with another Initiator, and two Responders are mismatched with each other. That is, like is mismatched with like. The same behaviour type is in conflict with itself. Two Initiators are always (often unconsciously) in competition, which has given rise to the expression 'Too many chiefs and not enough Indians'. Similarly, two Responders will also clash, as each will always be waiting for the other to take the initiative.

Two Responders will keep self-deprecatingly trying to allow the other person the right of way.

Initiators are good at starting things up, challenging the status quo, motivating, and stimulating action. They are strong leaders suited for command and authoritative leadership positions. They take charge when things are tough. They make things happen. They do well when working alone. However, while they are good at initiating things, they are not so reliable at following things through to the end. They are generally not completers, especially for very long-drawn-out tasks. Initiators can be, or become, dogmatic or autocratic leaders.

Responders are excellent at taking someone's initiative and running with it. They often develop or embellish a concept into something quite comprehensive. Many inventors are Initiators while their general managers are Responders. A great example is McDonald's hamburger chain. The McDonald brothers invented a great product concept and Ray Kroc turned it into a worldwide empire.

EXERCISE – INITIATOR/RESPONDER INTERACTIONS

Make some notes regarding important Initiator/Responder interactions you have had as a leader.

Important Initiator/Responder interactions I have had as a leader include

_____
_____
_____
_____
_____
_____
_____
_____
_____
_____
_____
_____
_____
_____
_____
_____
_____
_____
_____
_____
_____

USING YOUR ID PROFILE TO MATCH OTHERS' COMMUNICATION

First, assess your ID profile in relation to the other person. These three steps will help:

1. Identify the two dimensions that are most prominent in the way that you communicate when you are under pressure. For example, you may notice that when things get tough you tend to become more Rapid and Linear in your communication.

2. Contrast these two dimensions with the person with whom you're having the conversation. Consider how much you are like them on these two dimensions. Are you having difficulties or misunderstandings? Do you feel as though you are talking at cross-purposes?

    Based on your experience of them in the past and on your experience during the current conversation, if you assess that they are unlike you, you can be reasonably sure that they are opposite to you on these two aspects. For example, if you become more Rapid and Linear under stress, and the conversation is not working very comfortably, it is likely that they are Gradual and Lateral in their communication.

4. Mirror them as best you can. For example, if you are Rapid and Linear, slow down, be more patient, and pause more often. Stop being quite so step-by-step, be more flexible, and follow their ideas for a little bit.

Of course, this process works in the same manner with each of the Six Dimensions.

EXAMPLE – MATCHING OPPOSITE DIMENSIONS

Put an asterisk next to those you feel you will use.

If you are Rapid you often want to cut to the chase, and have things dealt with and finished.

How Rapids can match with Graduals

• deliberately speak more clearly and correctly.

• put your hands in your pockets or on your lap.

• breathe deeply and regularly.

• closely observe the other person.

• silently count to five between each sentence.

• sit still for some of the time.

• double your requested delivery timelines.

• think of snails.

• consider that Graduals are probably smarter than they seem.

• think of the countryside.

• speak more carefully.

• use language such as 'gradually', 'slowly', 'in time', 'when it's convenient for you', and 'there's no hurry'.

• have a Gradual colleague help you.

• delegate the task to a Gradual colleague.

• consider the other person is hiding their speed for some reason.

• think of the last bungle you made by being too hasty.

• think about world peace.

If you are Gradual you want to be sure all the information is provided carefully and accurately.

How Graduals can match with Rapids

- speak a little bit more quickly.
- move around a little.
- use language such as 'fast', 'quickly', 'short-term', 'rapid response'.
- delegate the task to a Rapid.
- think of racing cars.
- use some quick movements and actions.
- think of how important the meeting is to you.
- imagine that the other person is a little nervous and that's why they are speaking so quickly.
- imagine you are really late and in a desperate hurry.
- appreciate their level of energy.

If you are an Exaggerator you tend to present ideas in a larger-than-life way.

How Exaggerators can match with Understaters

- lower your voice a little.
- speak a little more slowly.
- dress a little more conservatively.
- make more ambiguous statements and fewer definite statements
- use language such as 'sort of', 'probably', 'mostly', 'sometimes', and 'a little'.
- sit still.

• use some neutral-coloured props in your presentation.
   • delegate the task to a Understater.
   • Make less eye contact.
   • tone down your exuberance.
   • think of cows.
   • be a little uncertain.
   • imagine the other person is restraining themselves in their exuberance.
   • imagine yourself to be smaller and less important than you are
   • imagine yourself to be a very humble person.

If you are an Understater you can be hard to read as you often minimise and downplay things.

How Understaters can match with Exaggerators

   • speak a little louder.
   • dress a little more dramatically.
   • move around a little during your presentation.
   • use colourful and/or noisy props.
   • delegate tasks to an Exaggerator.
   • think of a peacock on display.
   • make more eye contact (look at the other person's cheekbone if
   • you prefer—it will look like you're making eye contact without you having to do so).

• use language such as like 'definitely', 'absolutely', 'completely', and 'utterly'.

• think of one dramatic or flamboyant thing that you could do in that encounter.

• think of how important the encounter really is to you.

• imagine that the other person is a little insecure and that's why they are making dramatic and flamboyant statements and gestures.

• imagine yourself to be bigger and even more important than you are.

• imagine yourself to be a famous person.

If you are Linear you present in an ordered, sequential manner.

How Linears can match with Laterals

• deliberately speak less clearly and less precisely.

• dress down a little.

• be more flexible.

• change directions occasionally.

• move about a little.

• take one suggestion in five and see where it goes.

• think of Cook, Columbus, and discoveries.

• accept interjections.

• consider that Laterals are probably smarter than they seem

• make a few errors.

- use language such as 'sort of', 'kind of', 'sometimes', 'pretty much', 'I'm not sure', and 'maybe'.
- have a Lateral colleague help you.
- delegate the task to a Lateral colleague.
- imagine you are having fun.
- think of the last time you laughed at yourself.
- think of face painting and watching caterpillars.

If you are Lateral you often come at things in an open-ended, scattered fashion.

How Laterals can match with Linears
- speak a little more correctly with excellent pronunciation.
- be still more often.
- use language such as 'first', 'next', 'precisely', 'definitely', 'no', and 'absolutely'.
- delegate the task to a Linear.
- think of staying on the tracks.
- think in a straight line.
- arrive on time.
- end on time.
- do everything in the correct order.
- think of how important the meeting is to you.
- imagine that the other person is worried and that's why they are speaking so carefully.
- imagine you are in control.
- appreciate their level of control.

If you are a Detailer you are concerned about the specifics of the matter and pinpoint the details.

How Detailers can match with Conceptualisers

- pair up with a Conceptualiser.
- take a larger perspective.
- group small details into larger chunks.
- let go of the little bits and pieces.
- closely observe the other person.
- think about what is needed to hold all the little bits together.
- use language such as 'imagine', 'sort of', and 'out of left field'.
- look at the background, not just the foreground.
- study and read about abstract art.
- look at the Sydney Opera House.
- think landscape, not portrait.

If you are a Conceptualiser you concentrate on the big picture or bottom line.

How Conceptualisers can match with Detailers

- speak a little more precisely.
- make notes while you are conversing.
- use language such as 'precisely', 'in point of fact', 'specifically', and 'exactly'.
- delegate the task to a Detailer.
- think of little tiny bits.
- think basic elements.
- make lists.

- think of how important the meeting is to you.
- imagine that the other person is really excited by the idea.
- appreciate their level of intensity.
- think of the acoustic problems with the Sydney Opera House.

If you are a Self-Evaluator you tend to blame yourself and can be apologetic about getting what you want.

How Self-evaluators can match with Other-evaluators

- speak more curtly.
- be less flexible.
- stand a little closer to people than normal.
- speak up when you disagree.
- be a little more critical of others.
- consider that Other-evaluators are probably softer than they seem.
- accept no interjections.
- make sharp, short sentences.
- use language such as 'no', 'impossible', 'silly', and 'unbelievable'.
- use a tighter, sharper voice tone.
- have an Other-evaluator help you.
- delegate the task to an Other-evaluator.
- imagine you are a literary critic.
- suck on lemons before meetings.
- think of being a hanging judge on the bench.

If you are an Other-Evaluator you take a more removed or critical view of problems.

How Other-evaluators can match with Self-evaluators

• speak a little more quietly.

• consider other people's feelings before speaking.

• use language such as 'empathy', 'sorry', 'understanding', 'kindness', and 'consideration'.

• delegate the task to a Self-evaluator.

• think 'acceptance' and 'thoughtfulness'.

• smile.

• use a softer voice tone.

If you are an Initiator you take charge early on and are likely to clash with another Initiator.

How Initiators can match with Responders

• wait.

• slow down a little.

• ask other people for their ideas.

• be curious about pauses.

• ask for help.

• keep your eyes down.

• accept interjections.

• use language such as 'What shall we do now?', 'That's a good idea', and 'What else do you suggest?'

• have a Responder help you.

• delegate the task to a Responder.

• be willing to hear from others first.

• observe the group dynamics.

• think of the feelings and needs of everyone in the group.

• observe the facial expressions and voice tones of everyone in the group.

If you are a Responder you others take charge early on and hold back on putting forward what you want.

How Responders can match with Initiators

• think beforehand, and speak first.

• take charge.

• delegate the task to an Initiator.

• think of being the boss.

• think of being right.

• fill every silence with a suggestion.

• look up and forward.

• when in doubt, tell someone to make a suggestion.

• say 'I know we can do it, here's what I think'.

• imagine that the other person is worried and that's why they are speaking so carefully.

• imagine you are in control.

• appreciate the other person's level of control.

These last few pages have taken you through some suggestions about how your own Six Dimensions might be modified a little in order to better influence someone who has the opposite dimensions to you. They may stimulate you to identify people and situations where making modifications to your behaviour may be useful. Consider that you don't have to be at the complete opposite of someone in order to mismatch. Someone who is very rapid may still mismatch with other, less extreme Rapids.

ELECTRONIC ID

So far, we have been discussing how to communicate in face-to-face contexts. Yet many of our encounters involve written communication. The same approach to being empathic is also true for written communication.

To illustrate:

- Rapid/Gradual.

    You can write a Rapid email that is terse, brief, and uses dot points. Alternatively, you can write a Gradual email that rambles through the story, going off on tangents, until you arrive at your point in the fullness of time.

- Exaggerate/Understate.

    You can write an Exaggerated email filled with drama and 'we are all going to die' hyperbole. Or perhaps, you could possibly compose an Understated message with qualifiers. Maybe. Although it might be somewhat vague.

- Linear/Lateral.

    You could write an email that lays out the rules and gives lists of steps people need to follow. On the other hand, you could write a Lateral email that is more brainstorming and diffuse in style.

- Conceptualiser/Detailer.

    Your Conceptuliser email can focus on the big picture or grand vision. Alternatively, your Detailer email may discuss the specifics of your idea.

- Self-Evaluator/Other-Evaluator.

    You may write a self-effacing, 'Shucks, maybe I have this wrong but...' type of email. Or your email could be crafted as a 'You have got this wrong...' message.

- Initiate/Respond.

    You may take the lead in your email, stating, 'I suggest we do things this way...' Otherwise, your email could be more passive, 'I'd be interested to know what you think about...'

Matching the style of your written communication to the recipient's ID profile can initiate a process that leads to you being more influential.

I mentioned cross-cultural matching in the last chapter. The Influence Dimensions Test is designed as a culturally neutral instrument. Having used Influence Dimensions profiling in China, Indonesia, the Phillipines, the US, and Australia we can affirm anecdotally that matching and mismatching exists in all the dimensions, and is identical within the same culture. Between different cultures, the dimensions are impacted by context. For example, someone who is seen as an exaggerator within the context of Indonesian culture is likely to be viewed as an Understater within the context of American culture.

HOW TO FURTHER ENHANCE YOUR INFLUENTIAL LEADERSHIP

Having some status or authority helps. People will follow the lead of credible, knowledgeable experts. Is there a respected authority, other than yourself, that you can refer to in conversation to add more credibility to your goal? Further, does your message confirm or contradict those you are addressing? You will be more influential if you point to an agreed code or belief system that incorporates your message.

The amygdala panics when you are not consistent and quite linear in your message. If you need to make a diversion, prepare your audience for the shift and explain why you are taking them in a different direction.

Be nice. People prefer to say yes to folks they like. How can you reinforce this during the conversation? If you aren't well-liked by the person or people you are addressing, how can you minimise the impact?

SUMMARY OF INFLUENCE SKILLS

- Watch and listen.
- Know your own ID profile comprehensively.
- Match with Planner/Analyser or Creator/Developer styles.
- Identify your two strongest dimensions and modify them if you are not connecting well.
- Thoughtfully, subtlety, use language, tone of voice, and non-verbal behaviours that match with the other person's ID profile.

6

RESPECTING

"If you go looking for a friend, you're going to find they're very scarce. If you go out to be a friend, you'll find them everywhere."

– Zig Ziglar

This is a potent part of your empathy development. Without a level of self-respect and respect for others we cannot be influential leaders.

You are in control of your own value and worth. Others may criticise you, but you do not have to accept it.

Empathy towards another is only as effective as the empathy you have towards yourself.

You do not have to like everyone, but communicating with people you don't like very much requires more effort than mere compliance. You need to work on building some level of respect for them *inside your own mind*.

If you smile and play nice, but mentally harbour your issue with them, it will show. Unless you are in an online Zoom meeting, you don't see your face – you're inside it – but in any face-to-face situation the other person sees it. If you are holding onto negative feelings then your facial expressions and body language will give you away, whether it's your knitted brow, your tight hands, your stiff neck, or your constricted voice. In order to be influential, you need to work hard at developing some genuine respect for them.

When you value your relationships more than your ego, then it is easier to let go of the need to always be right. Compassion is a core feature of respect, and has been shown to improve trust. Compassion is hard to fake and difficult to build in one conversation. Nonetheless, the more you can access compassion for others, the more successful you will be in gaining their respect and trust.

Being understood and understanding others is a necessary means for achieving compassion. Knowing something about other peoples' worldviews, assumptions, values, and expectations will assist you in being familiar, trustworthy, influential, and compassionate. Compassion is not a feeling some of us have and others don't. It is a product of skilful observation and matching.

Positive recognition is an internal mindset with external benefits. It establishes an openness to gratitude – for oneself and others. Merely being grateful for what you have makes you a better leader. It is appreciative empathy. Negative recognition is an internal mindset that accumulates blame and criticism, and does not inspire respect.

THE RECOGNITION GRID

The Recognition Grid vividly maps out the trust building and trust-busting results of the way we give feedback. In short, you will be a more influential leader if you create positive relationships with others. Your primitive brain stores positives and negatives cumulatively. It loves negatives more.

Success usually starts way before you need it. Certainly, giving negative feedback for a long time and then suddenly being 'nice' isn't the way to build a positive relationship.

The nature of feedback provided by a leader has a dramatic effect on others' motivation and willingness to support you. This feedback may be provided verbally or non-verbally. However, it always needs to be genuine.

The four types of recognition are:
• Generalised positive.
• Specific positive.
• Specific negative.
• Generalised negative.

A **generalised positive** is a comment like, 'You're good to work with' or 'I appreciate you'. It applies to the person and is not specifically connected to any behaviour. A non-verbal display of unconditional support, such as a pat on the back or a warm smile, is also a general positive.

A **specific positive** is a comment like, 'Thanks for helping me with that job yesterday' or 'I'm glad you got that to me so quickly'. It applies directly to a good task or action the person has done and is only half as potent as a general positive.

A **specific negative** is a comment like, 'You didn't help much yesterday!' or 'This isn't done properly!' In this case, the performance is poor and is being clearly pointed out. This feedback is clearly a demotivation.

The final type of recognition is the **generalised negative.** This includes expressions like 'You're hopeless!' or 'You're impossible to work with', or non-verbal actions such as ignoring the person altogether. This is directed at the whole person and is not limited to a particular behaviour or action. As such, it causes the most serious level of demotivating force.

It is clear from this model that negatives are always more potent and are remembered far longer than positives. Also, because of this, it is easy to lower morale, simply because of a lack of attention to the nature of your feedback.

Now here's the kicker...

Generalised positive recognition is worth +100 Angstrom units of motivating force.

This recognition is necessary for self-esteem, self-confidence, and creativity. It encourages innovation and risk-taking, and builds trust. The person doesn't have to behave in any particular way to deserve this acknowledgement – they are just appreciated for who they are.

Specific positive recognition is worth +50 Angstrom units of motivating force.

This occurs when a good action or behaviour is specifically recognised. It has half the potency of generalised positivity because it depends on the person doing a good action. In order to receive more, you need to deliver more.

Specific negative recognition is worth −200 Angstrom units of motivating force.

This feedback is corrective and occurs when the person makes a mistake or performs poorly.

Both specific positive recognition and specific negative recognition are needed for training people in new tasks. Specific negative recognition is often easier to provide, yet is quite demotivating. Specific positive recognition is more rewarding but usually requires more patience and tolerance.

Generalised negative recognition is worth a whopping −1000 Angstrom units of motivating force.

This usually scares people into short-term performance improvement, but it quickly causes demoralisation and reduced wellbeing. This type of feedback damages self-esteem and confidence.

Many leaders give almost no credit when people do more than they were supposed to do, for going that extra mile, but they are quick to punish people for what they haven't done, or what they have done incorrectly.

In one experiment, a helper assisted participants do a complex task. If the helper provided much more assistance than promised, participants gave them the same rating as if the helper had just done the basic job. If the helper did a really poor job, the participants were really critical. Herein is a great lesson for leaders – don't make promises you don't keep. The negative reaction will last longer than if you delivered on the promise.

People learn more quickly when threats are used, as opposed to rewards, *but onlyin the short-term.* After that, productivity, morale, and trust are eroded, and you have a poor workplace culture.

In contrast, research has revealed how recognition from a manager can give a powerful lift in the culture overall. Motivating recognition requires the manager to engage in three actions:
- having candid conversations.
- defining clear and relevant performance goals.
- holding people accountable for their results.

These three actions capture the foundation of influential communication – respectful honesty, clear focus, and responsibility.

Self-respect needs to be in the bedrock of leadership. Without it, every other skill can so easily fall over. However, it is very common for people to be secretly, persuasively, self-critical.

Without acknowledging that we have any inadequacies we are liars, and smug. Our self-criticism can keep us humble and questioning our rightness and arrogance. However, too much insecurity renders us inadequate and troubled.

Inadequacy and self-criticism arises out of the moral framework of your parents and teachers, where good behaviour was often encouraged largely through fear of punishment for bad behaviour.

Once again, your leadership development is dragged kicking and screaming through the minefield of your personal assumptions. You need to change your personal self-criticism in order to be less self-critical of your leadership abilities.

In pursuit of your goal to become a more empathetic and influential leader, you may find that some behaviours are not the best strategies. These behaviours need to be recognised and comfortably realigned.

Perfectionism is often the bag in which many of us carry our self-criticism. It fits in pretty snugly. Let me share a little of my own perfectionist journey.

EXAMPLE – PRESENT IMPERFECT

My apprenticeship to be a card-carrying perfectionist was pretty placid. All I did was watch my Whyalla Shipyard labourer father start his own business, build his own house, learn to fly an aeroplane, be a maths genius, and beat me in every tennis game we played, on the tennis court that he had perfectly built. He was generally an all-round star.

All I did was to emulate this in everything I did.

When I was thirty-two, I bought a 150-year-old cottage and rebuilt the bathroom and kitchen from the earth floor upwards. I fitted an exquisitely tiled bathroom with fancy shower and built-in bathtub. The kitchen oven and fridge were installed, the sink plumbed, the cupboards built-in, the floor tiled, and the glass splash-back fitted. It was straight out of Home Beautiful.

You'd think by this stage of my life I would have learnt my lesson, but no, I needed approval for being an excellent handyman, and so I invited my dad to inspect the kitchen. It was such a good job that I wasn't worried at all. He came in, glanced around the kitchen, picked up the spirit level, placed it on the bench edge of one of the cabinets and said, 'Ah – a drop of one in fifty. Pity you didn't level it.'

My next perfectionist event happened a year after that visit.

I needed some gas fitters to install a heater in the lounge room. They came and installed the heater and did the copper tubing around the skirting board out to the gas tank. As they were starting to nail the skirting board back in place, to cover the gas piping, I said, 'No don't worry about it, I'll put those back in.'

They left.

Smugly, confidently, I was halfway through nailing them all back in, when psssssstttt. Escaping gas from the neat hole I had drilled into the gas pipe.

Talk about self-criticism. I went off my head. I yelled and shouted abuse at myself. I couldn't call them back, it would be too humiliating, but I couldn't fix it myself. When I finally stopped ranting and had a beer, I discovered that I had spent two-and-a-half hours abusing myself for making a simple mistake. That was my perfectionism wake up call.

Since then I have only had occasional bursts of being perfect. Mostly, I'm satisfied with a pretty modest level of professionalism. I am also a nicer leader, as a result.

Self-respect means having boundaries for your dealings with other people. You need to value and hold to those boundaries, and make them clear to others. Self-respect requires you to negotiate your boundaries with the boundaries of others. This is where you ensure you are behaving in an ethical way. You are manoeuvring between being true to yourself whilst also respecting others.

To be responsible in this way means understanding that it's not what happens to you that matters, but what you do with it. You need self-awareness and trust in yourself. You need to take responsibility for your decisions rather than blaming others.

Self-respect is personal. This is where the assumptions you worked on in Chapter Three come into play. Somewhere in your history you decided you were worthy or not so worthy as a person. This occurred without a conscious choice because you were still developing a complex brain. This means you made a really big assumption with no supporting data. It was just a primitive brain generalisation. Since then, in the weird way of things, you will have engaged in behaviours and actions to either support your worthiness, or to try to prevent the bad consequences of being unworthy. The first builds and enables self-respect. The second, paradoxically, builds and reinforces a lack of self-respect.

If your history supported the first, you have a great start on being an empathetic and influential leader. If the second path dominated, you need to re-deicide your early assumption.

EXERCISE – SELF-RESPECT RE-DECISION ROUTINE

Questions And Tips

Take a few minutes to go through the following points.

1. What qualities do your friends say you have? List them here, even if you don't agree:

....
....
....
....
....
....
....
....

2. If you dismiss these as true qualities, in what ways does this happen, and why?

....
....
....
....
....
....
....
....

3. Forgive yourself. Again. And again. And again.

4. Watch people who get an A+ for self-respect.

5. Treat others with respect.

6. Don't allow others to disrespect you.

7. Be consistent with everything you do.

8. Review and assess what you say in your head. Just notice it.

9. Do some counselling on your negative assumptions. You don't need them anymore.

10. You are valuable for being you.

Self-respect, far more than self-esteem, is essential for leadership. Self-worth derives from compassion. A good leader is compassionate towards others, and a great leader is compassionate towards themselves.

Self-compassion means treating yourself with kindness, even when you feel inadequate.

You can ask yourself three questions when you feel you have done something wrong.

1. How many people have had a similar bad experience?

2. If a close friend had this experience, what advice would you give them?

3. How would a neutral observer view the situation that is causing you to judge yourself?

By asking yourself these questions, you may well realise that you're not the only one who makes mistakes and encounters negative experiences. As a result, you're less likely to ruminate on it and use those events to measure your sense of self-worth.

Self-compassion makes us stronger emotionally, not weaker or less influential. Being kind to yourself doesn't equate to being self-pitying.

RESPECTING OTHERS

Find at least one thing about the other person you could admire. If you are struggling to see their admirable qualities, consider this list:

- They try hard.
- They persevere.
- They have strong beliefs.

- They are loyal to their cause.
- They stand up to you.

The overarching contributor to being an influential leader is your ability to use your Emotional Intelligence. Self-respect and respect for others are connected to your Emotional Quotient. As we discussed in Chapter 2, your EQ determines your ability to understand and regulate emotions, and to continue to grow and develop emotionally, which is why EQ is widely regarded as the essential leadership quality.

EQ is an individual's ability to accurately recognise, understand and manage their own emotions as well as those of others. It is a fundamental leadership skill.

EQ is not personality based. A quiet introvert can have an extremely high EQ. A noisy extrovert can have an extremely high EQ. Emotional intelligence is a learned behaviour. The good news is that it isn't all that much hard work. It simply requires a commitment to change.

EMOTIONAL INTELLIGENCE – AN OVERVIEW

This is the common view of Emotional Intelligence, which was popularised by Daniel Goleman.[11]

Self-Awareness is the most important element, as every other quality depends on this. You need to be aware of your emotions, strengths, limitations, and behaviours – and to understand how these affect those around you.

Given the brain/body/emotion interconnection, self-awareness also means that you have an acute sense of what your body is telling you – the tense shoulders, itchy feet, and shallow breathing are all messages to which it is good to pay attention. Self-awareness also enables a sense of humour, which is a vastly underrated leadership quality. When you are self-aware, you are more likely to be confident and to know how other people regard you.

Self-Management – by managing your emotions you are able to prevent amygdala driven reactions.

Self-management means picking the right time and place to say what you feel. You express your emotions appropriately in the context of the matter. This means making your amygdala be quiet, and using the prefrontal cortex to run stuff. You are then being adaptable and flexible. Difficult conversations are easier when you are able to self-regulate. This means you are responsible and care about your behaviour.

Pull Motivation

You need to *want* to use your EQ skills to be an influential leader. This means committing to using these skills all the time and not just when it suits you.

Empathy – is a central aspect in your quest for influential leadership. All the previous chapters have reinforced this element of EQ.

People Skills – these help you connect with an endless variety of colleagues, bosses, and clients.

You do not have to be an extrovert, charismatic, or outgoing to be effective with people. Matching is using people skills. Listening is using people skills. Being polite is using people skills. Giving recognition and support is using people skills. You can be a good communicator by interpreting ideas in your team and being available. In general, when you have good people skills, you are able to practise being open to good and bad news.

WHAT IS EQ?

EQ is focused on recognising, understanding, and using your emotions effectively. Emotions often have different root causes. Most individuals are not able to clearly identify their emotions, the causes of their emotions, and how to manage them.

Research studies have asked people to write down names of emotions they can recognise in themselves and others. The mean number of emotions that people can identify is four – mad (angry), sad, bad (scary), and glad (happy).

A high EQ person can distinguish – in others and themselves – at least five layers of nuance for each of these four basic emotions. For example, a little annoyed, quite upset, very disturbed, furious, homicidal. This distinction clearly gives an influential advantage to the leader over simply recognising the emotion as 'bad'.

We are talking about EQ in the context of leadership, so it may not come as a surprise to know that recent research suggests Emotional Intelligence diminishes as people move up the corporate ladder, and that CEOs have the lowest EQ scores in the workplace!

Why does this happen?

If you study CEOs, MDs, and senior leaders, you see they operate in a different environment from middle managers. Senior leaders spend more time in formal meetings, more time with leadership peers with whom they are often competing, and less time in meaningful human vulnerable chats with their staff.

They have climbed the ladder of responsibility to step onto the shaky platform of entitlement. They become more out of touch with the impact of their behaviour on others, and more shielded from exposure to their vulnerabilities.

Almost everyone suffers from insecurity, and the fear of not being good enough. We all try to disguise this in one way or another. Many people do not like to be open and vulnerable, and so the response is to bluster, bully, deny, and over-perform.

This often represents the 'imposter syndrome' bias. You feel like a fraud and constantly question your ability. You know that any second now, you will be found out. This insecurity becomes more vital to hide the more senior you become. The citadel walls of defence you build mean your EQ is more hidden away, and so it atrophies.

Emotional Intelligence means having the confidence to meet your own needs as well as fulfilling the demands of your external responsibilities. Where there is a disparity between the two, Emotional Intelligence requires acknowledging your shortcomings, and letting other people know where your limits lie. When you do this, you are leading with emotional maturity.

In our childhoods, we are often either given free range to emotional outbursts or discouraged from emotional expression. This is how we form some of our big assumptions, and create other defences against being vulnerable and unsafe.

Showing respect is a good way to be influential but use discernment in your assessment of people. Be open and accepting at first, observe and learn. If the respect is abused, try Plan B. Showing the other person how they're right is a shrewd way of gaining influence while still being respectful. This the essence of the principle that the best way to help people change their own minds is to first show them how they are right.

Telling someone they're wrong will only tap into the other person's resistance, and fix them more firmly in their beliefs. Instead, listen carefully, be curious about their ideas, and match their mindset. They need to shift from their long-held assumptions and beliefs on their own.

To change someone's mind, you need to address their emotional attachment to what they believe. Take a step back and truly try to understand the other person's perspective and validate his or her point of view. Once you have done this you can then work with them to arrive at your desired outcome or solution.

With more listening, and less trying to get the other person to submit to your will, their defences are much more likely to come down. It is a matter of short-term ego versus long-term influence.

Your brain is a pattern-recognition machine. It makes observations and starts forming rules about the world. Sometimes however, your brain makes errors when it's forming its rules. For example, if you were made fun of in primary school during 'Show and Tell' then an early big assumption could be that, 'Speaking to a large group is terrifying' – the conclusion to this would be 'I will never do it again'.

These old, hardened paths in our brain form automatic thoughts that have a negative impact on EQ and influential leadership.

EQ IS CONSTRAINED BY OUR LIMITING THOUGHTS

We all have doubts about ourselves. These self-doubts limit our ability and constrain our EQ. Here are some of our favourite EQ downers:

Making everything black and white, right and wrong – using the rating system from Chapter Two allows for better ongoing conversations. For instance, 'I think you have this about 8/10 correct, let's discuss the 2/10 bit'.

The amygdala loves to clump data but making broad conclusions based on little evidence is an emotional trigger. Words such as 'all', 'every', 'none', 'never', 'always', and 'impossible' are not useful.

Confirmation bias – when you see a person and you assume you know what they are thinking or feeling. For example, 'That smirk proves George disagrees with me.'

Essentially, being a drama queen is a great EQ buster. Don't sweat the small stuff. And remember – it's all small stuff.

'Shoulds' and 'Oughts' – these are the nagging voices that always stir up resistance and reaction. They are often part of our big assumptions. To counter this you probably need to go back to your Three Leadership Steps and revise the rules a little.

Remember – you are accountable and responsible for yourself. Other people aren't frustrating you – your own expectations are. Change them.

It's helpful to keep in mind that not everyone has the same values as you.

Being an influential leader is fairly straightforward when you are dealing with people you like and with whom you share the same values. As an influential leader, you also need to connect well with people whose values clash with your own beliefs. To be effective in achieving this requires lots of preparation, careful re-examination of your own values and ethics, and sophisticated reframing.

EXAMPLE – RE-EXAMINING AND REFRAMING VALUES

I worked with a colleague once on a professional board. Some of his beliefs about women and race were appalling to me. We had argued extensively over the years, but now we needed to resolve a major action for our board. I started doing my homework about him. I read about his journey, which involved pushing against many obstacles. I noted that his peers often elected him to important roles, which showed they respected and recognised his abilities.

At our next meeting I offered him the seat at the head of the table. I matched his attire and presentation, and started by saying, 'Fred, despite all our differences I need to say I admire your tenacity and perseverance.' That was enough for me to be even-handed and for him to be more moderately tenacious.

THE PRIMITIVE BRAIN DRIVERS AFFECTING YOUR LEADERSHIP

There are several areas of human social interaction that can impact on you being influential. These are areas where your amygdala gets super-sensitive. This is a reflexive activity. Clearly, this response is not the ideal state of affairs when conducting valuable conversations. However, this response is the default situation that often occurs. Your brain is more attuned to threats than rewards. The threat response is often just below the surface and is very easily triggered – by the wrong look, gesture, or word.

The feeling of being in control is a biggie. We like to know we are running things and leading from the front. If we are being criticised or being told off, the fight/flight routine gets a workout and we stop being so influential.

Providing the other person with a genuine sense of control is worth the effort if you wish to be influential. Genuine efforts of matched non-verbal and ID Dimension conversation are beneficial.

Being involved and feeling you are in charge can be make or break for some serious leadership conversations. One way to do this is by enabling the relevant people to be fully involved in the discussion. People feel more in control when they believe you understand where they are coming from. They feel more secure when they are learning and improving, and when attention is paid to this improvement.

Feeling in control increases when people are given positive feedback, especially public acknowledgement. This is very significant during and after a difficult conversation (see the Recognition Grid).

There is a cunning little routine from Ericksonian therapy called the **double bind.** It's a technique that engages the other person in the process and offers them some alternatives, while still heading in the direction you think is important.

For example, if you know that Steve is hesitant about a new project, you could ask, 'Steve, would you like to select your own team for the new project, or would you prefer to work with a team that I select?'

The action of Steve doing the project is assumed, but he has choice and collaboration on the type of team he might work with.

As parents of young kids my wife and I encountered bedtime tantrums. Susan and I tried this double bind with great success. 'Peter – would you like to go to bed now or after watching Sesame Street?' Being a smart kid he chose after. Unexpected and unusual situations also muck us around. If it feels different or out of the ordinary it immediately catches your amygdala's attention. The brain likes to know the pattern that is occurring moment-to-moment. It craves certainty, so that some prediction is possible. Without prediction, the brain must use dramatically more resources. Even a small amount of uncertainty generates an 'error' response which takes attention away from one's goals, forcing attention to the error. This reduces effective thinking and learning.

Meeting expectations generates an increase in dopamine levels in the brain, which is a reward response. Matching ensures clarity and familiarity, and generates certainty.

Uncertainty can be decreased in many simple ways, including:

- Establishing clear expectations of what might happen in the conversation, as well as expectations of desirable outcomes.
- Breaking down the conversation into transparent aspects.

Lack of fairness is the top complaint from most people about any important conversations.

Unfair exchanges generate a strong threat response. This causes activation of the amygdala and generates intense emotions such as disgust.

It's beneficial to examine if you are being fair about a matter, or if you might be perceived as unfair.

The threat from perceived unfairness can be reduced by:

- Increasing transparency, and the level of communication and involvement about the issues.
- Establishing clear expectations in all parts of the conversation.
- Providing clear ground rules and expectations.

David Rock detailed similar aspects in his SCARF model.[12]

TOP TIP

You can increase a person's sense of safety simply by sitting next to them.

SUMMARY OF RESPECT SKILLS

- See people as worthy, at least at first.
- See yourself as worthy, and keep working at it.
- Re-educate yourself to understand that mistakes are OK.
- Search for something you can admire in the other person.
- Maintain but modify your expectations.

7

REFRAMING

**'Reality is what we take to be true.
What we take to be true is what we
believe. What we believe determines
what we take to be true.'**

– David Bohm

There is a great cartoon that exquisitely shows reframing in action.

It pictures a lone knight on a battlefield surrounded by hundreds of dead soldiers with arrows sticking out of them. Sword raised aloft, he proclaims to the enemy, 'Now we have all your arrows!'

There is also a wonderful real-life example of reframing. Until the 1968 Olympics the 'Straddle Method' was the way everyone performed the high jump. However, there was nothing in the rulebook to say that the Straddle Method *had* to be used. This meant that when the American Dick Fosbury literally turned things on their head by jumping backwards over the bar and increasing the height that could be cleared, he made a name for himself in the history books. Since then, everyone uses the Fosbury Flop.

THE ART OF REFRAMING

Reframing is another brilliant leadership technique. Essentially, reframing, is about problem solving.

As a leadership skill, reframing is polite, respectful redirection. Reframing enables you to accept the other person's interpretation and offer them another way of viewing the same matter. It virtually eliminates resistance and builds rapport. Saying, 'No, you're wrong' or, 'This is the way to do it' may seem easier, but in the context of long-term gains, it is a losing option. Reframing is harder, as you need to pause and think first.

Reframing may be considered as an act of interpretation. A matter may be interpreted in several ways, unless we are being dogmatic. Taking a person's interpretation and suggesting an allied but different interpretation is reframing.

Reframing also has biological roots. We frame our life according to our upbringing and experience. We make distinctions between things – some elements are included, some remain in the background. This frame then shapes our perceptions, which reinforces our framed view.

Our frame is a product of the unique interaction of our nervous system and its environment. What we frame is our picture. It is framed by the moment and is available to be reframed, or redefined, whenever suitable changes occur in our environment.

Frames that are created in this way can be extinguished when new distinctions are made. People only change their behaviour in interaction with their environment. Framing can be very subtle, but it is always consequential. If your frame is too broad, focus can be lost. If your frame is too narrow, the context is ignored. If the frame is too big and too ornate it can overshadow the picture inside.

Another cartoon shows two prisoners in a jail cell. Both are painting pictures. One captures in colourful detail the trees, sunshine, and birds flying past outside the window. The other paints the window bars. Neuroendocronologist, Robert Sapolsky said, 'If you pay lots of attention to where boundaries are, you pay less attention to the complete picture.'[13]

YOU'VE BEEN FRAMED

As a leader, you will introduce people to work tasks, new projects, difficult conversations, and organisational changes. How you frame these introductions builds an expectant attitude. This will be positive or negative depending on your framing.

A leader's casual body language, turn of phrase, past expectations, or expressions can create a successful outcome or a failure. This is fact. How you frame things influences how they turn out.

Researchers have found that people are more likely to prefer options framed positively. For example, they are more likely to enjoy meat labelled 75 per cent lean as opposed to 25 per cent fat, or to use condoms advertised as being 95 per cent effective as opposed to having a 5 per cent risk of failure.

In the context of leadership, this means that you can literally frame motivation and engagement or resistance or demotivation.

When considering major activities, simple framing can shift the focus from short-term to long-term. When presented with task descriptions described in positive, negative, or neutral terms, managers are significantly more likely to agree to an approach when it is positively described than when it is described neutrally or negatively.

Additionally, framing often leads to inconsistency in choice. A change in framed descriptions after an initial agreement is made can cause managers to abandon their initial decision in favour of an alternative option. The research shows we all remember positively framed statements more accurately than negatively framed statements.

MATCHING AND REFRAMING

'Even the most well-intentioned and empathetic among us, are creatures invariably bound by frames

of reference, without vantage point confined to our own corner of reality.' –Popou

The process of matching is the cornerstone of reframing. It is a form of communication that lends itself to a more comprehensive fit with the other person's point of view.

The process by which 'adaptation' occurs requires a certain kind of matched communication which is malleable enough to evolve. This is the process of structural, or neuronal, coupling.

The process creates a new structure, which, because the two of you are matched, induces your counterpart to also adopt the new structure – or reframed point of view. Similarly, you will be more open to their point of view.

In terms of responsibilities and the concern about manipulation, it is important to understand that the reframed change occurs as a result of the other person's response to the reframed ideas. You do not and cannot cause the behaviour change. The other person maintains autonomy at the social, psychological, and biological level.

The nature of reframing has two elements. First, to offer an alternative viewpoint, and second, to make the offer in such a way that it will be accepted. This is only likely to occur when the person offering the alternative viewpoint matches the other person as closely as possible.

This enables influential leadership, and change. Matching without leading simply maintains the original viewpoint, while mismatching ends the conversation.

EXPERIMENT – TWO FINGERS ON THE TIP OF THE NOSE

Cross the index and middle finger of your preferred hand and touch the tip of your nose simultaneously with the two tips of the crossed fingers. If you do this you may feel that you have two nose tips, quite in contradiction with what the mirror tells you. If you are now asked whether you have one or two nose tips, you will say one or two according to whether you prefer the mirror or the crossed fingers as adequate evidence.

Most people prefer to accept the mirror, but this does not change the fact that accepting one experience over the other is a perception. With or without the mirror you experience two nose tips. The mirror, or other observers, provide you with information about only one nose tip.

WHAT IS REALITY?

For the most part, you take your reality for granted. And to a great extent you create the reality in which you exist by thinking it. You talk yourself into your worldview, or frame of reference. In the reality of science, such as quantum physics, an electron is both a particle *and* a wave at the same time – depending on the method of observation.

Going back to our discussion of distance and depth, your brain does not perceive distance as a part of the environment. You create distance as part of your neuronal function. The more plastic the structure of an organism, the more diversified modes of behaviour it can generate.

You frame most of your conversations, often unconsciously, by putting a barrier around what's in context and what isn't. You could change the frame by zooming out (expanding and enlarging the point of view by including more information inside the context) or zooming in (narrowing the point of view by constricting what's in context).

Expanding the frame allows for more lateral associations to be included in your thinking. These associations could offer other unconsidered alternatives. On the other hand, it could broaden the perspective so much that the trees are lost in the forest.

Constricting the frame can sharpen the focus and put a spotlight on the core issue. However, if the focus is on the wrong issue, or if there is more than one issue, then the framing will be unhelpful, and you may have missed your opportunity.

The skill is to decide which size frame best matches the person you wish to influence.

So how do you adjust the frame?

You may adjust the frame by using a particular word, a metaphor, a simile, humour, reinterpretation, or repetition.

Reframing is a communication technique that reduces resistance and increase flexibility in the other person. It develops the ability to regard a situation from different points of view and, therefore, helps the other person to be more amenable to change.

Due to the mass of data we have to process, your brain simplifies and reduces this data into understandable chunks. One of the ways we do this is by categorising things into distinct classes. The problem with this way of shaping our worldview is that once a matter is framed in a certain way, it is extremely difficult to see it also as belonging to another class.

For example, close questioning may be classed as criticism, and so the valid alternative class, 'curious', may be a blocked possibility. A gun may be classed as a killing weapon, and the class 'sporting fun' may be blanked out. Blankets may be classed as bed coverings, and so we may have trouble seeing them as 'forts'.

With reframing, when you are led to see an alternative class, it is difficult to go back to your previously restricted view of the matter. Reframing allows an idea or object to be thought of as fitting into a different category. You have expanded your frame of reference, and, therefore, your openness to change. Reframing enables flexibility and tolerance.

For effective reframing, the new category must fit the facts of the person and the situation as well, or better, than the one it replaces. In actuality, without such skilled matching, the reframed view is usually ignored.

Reframing can be tremendously helpful in problem solving, decision-making, and learning. It is a way of helping you, or another person, to more constructively move on from a situation in which they are stuck or confused. The aim of reframing is to shift one's perspective to be more empowered to act – and hopefully to learn at the same time.

As leaders we do not actually connect with facts. Our minds are stubborn, and so we quickly jump from, 'This sounds right to me' to 'This is true'.

Most facts have a half-life. So your questions point to the facts you believe. Think of questions as different camera lenses. Put on a wide-angle lens, and you'll capture the entire scene. Put on a zoom lens, and you'll get a close-up shot.

When you reframe a question by changing your method of questioning, you have the power to change the answers.

A great leader is great at problem-solving. More accurately, a great leader is great at providing an environment where problems get solved. They employ empathy, reframing, and matching as integral parts of solving problems at work.

Problem definition is the most critical step in *problem-solving.* A poorly analysed problem usually results in an excellent solution that doesn't work.

This is the point at which rescuing leaders need to beware! The urge for Rescuers to quickly leap to solutions before thoroughly determining the actual problem is very strong.

Before anything else, assess the nature of the problem. Is it a modest issue, which needs small adjustments from within the system? Or is it a more serious problem, requiring transformational change from outside the normal way of doing things?

We all tend to define problems from inside our own familiar frame of reference, so we may see it in one dimension only. We can end up devising a 'solution' that is familiar but doesn't actually solve anything. For significant organisation-wide challenges, a diverse problem-solving team can be amazingly successful. With widely different perspectives and experiences, such a team is able to bring diverse options to the matter – if they are well led.

You need IQ and EQ to be a problem-solving leader. You need to have accumulated experience about the world, and the people that inhabit it.

Most leadership problems are complex people problems occurring within a complex work system. We do not assist in resolving these problems with a neat 'here's your solution' delivery. Problems can only be understood, and therefore solved, by continuous interaction, trying out options, and making adjustments as more information is gathered.

FRONTAL LOBE PROBLEM-SOLVING

Defining the problem[14]

The first step is to correctly define the problem. Evidence indicates we muck-up this first crucial step very often. Definition involves diagnosing a situation so that the focus is on the real causes of the problem, not just its symptoms.

For example, suppose you must deal with an employee who consistently fails to get her work done on time. Slow work might be the root cause, or it might be only a symptom of another underlying problem such as poor health, low morale, lack of training, or inadequate rewards.

To solve the problem, a wide search for information is needed in order to help to pinpoint underlying causes. The more information acquired, the more likely it is that the problem will be defined accurately.

Here are some attributes of good problem definition for more influential leadership:

1. Factual information is differentiated from opinion or speculation. Objective data are separated from perceptions and suppositions.
2. A wide range of people is asked for information.
3. The problem is stated explicitly. The problem definition clearly identifies what standard or expectation has been violated. Problems, by their very nature, involve the violation of some standard or expectation.
4. The problem definition also needs to address who needs to take responsibility for resolving the problem. Identifying the wrong person results in a wrong solution.
5. The definition is not simply a disguised solution. Saying 'The problem is that we need to motivate slow employees' is inappropriate, because the problem is stated as a solution.
6. Managers often propose a solution before an adequate definition of a problem has been given. This may lead to solving the 'wrong' problem. Therefore, the definition step in problem-solving is extremely important.

Generating alternatives

The second step is to generate alternative solutions. This requires postponing the selection of any one solution until several alternatives have been proposed. We have known for many years that the quality of solutions can be significantly enhanced by considering multiple alternatives.

Rather than rushing into judgement too quickly, judgement and evaluation must be delayed so that the first acceptable solution suggested is not necessarily the one immediately selected.

A common problem in leadership decision-making is that alternatives are evaluated as they are proposed, so the first acceptable one is chosen, even if it is not the optimal solution.

Some tips for this second step are:

1. The evaluation of each proposed alternative is postponed.

2. Alternatives are proposed by all individuals involved in the problem.

3. Alternative solutions are consistent with organisational goals or policies.

4. Alternatives take into consideration both short-term and long-term consequences.

5. Alternatives build on one another. Bad ideas may become good ones if they are combined with, or modified by, other ideas.

6. Alternatives solve the problem that has been defined. Another problem may also be important, but it should be ignored if it does not directly affect the problem being considered.

Evaluating alternatives

The third step is to evaluate and select an alternative. This step involves careful weighing of the advantages and disadvantages of the proposed alternatives before making a final selection.

Highly influential leaders make sure that:

- alternatives will solve the problem without causing other unanticipated problems.
- all individuals involved will accept the alternative.
- the implementation of the alternative is likely.
- the alternative fits within organisational constraints, so that it is consistent with policies, norms, and budget limitations.
- the most conspicuous alternative is not selected without considering others.

Many leaders react to a problem by trying to implement a solution before they have defined it, analysed it, or generated and evaluated alternative solutions. Slow is better than fast in solving problems.

However, implementing any solution requires matching and influential communication with those who will be affected by it. Almost any change engenders some resistance. Therefore, the best leaders are careful to select a strategy that maximises the probability that the solution will be accepted and fully implemented.

Problems are the most common challenges to being an influential leader, and it too easy to take shortcuts. In my consultancy experience, as many as 70 per cent of leaders select quick and expedient over slow and lasting.

The 'small wins' concept is useful here. It involves implementing part of the solution that is easy to accomplish, and then publicising it. You then continue implementing incrementally to achieve small wins. This strategy decreases resistance, as small changes are usually not worth fighting over. It also creates support, as others observe progress (a bandwagon effect occurs) and reduces costs, as failure is not career-ending, and large allocations of resources are not required before success is assured. On top of this, it helps to ensure persistence and perseverance in implementation.

Effective implementation also requires follow-up, to prevent negative side effects and to ensure the problem has been solved. Few decisions work out the way they are intended to, and even the most effective decision may eventually become obsolete.

An analytical problem-solving model can work well, but is less effective with complex problems. These can include things such as discovering why staff morale is low, determining how to implement downsizing without antagonising employees, developing a new process that will increase productivity, and identifying ways to overcome resistance to change. These kinds of problems do not always have an easily identifiable definition or set of alternative solutions available.

Such problems require a new way of thinking – creative problem solving is the answer.

Creative problem-solving

Creative problem-solving is focused on generating something new. We have discussed our personal brain functions that block us at work and inhibit us from solving certain problems effectively.

These blocks are due to the generalisations about the world, which is how you manage when your brain is bombarded with far more information than we can possibly absorb. These filtering habits eventually become conceptual blocks that inhibit us from registering some kinds of information and therefore from solving certain kinds of problems.

Paradoxically, the more formal education individuals have, and the more experience they have in a job, the less able they are to solve problems in creative ways. It has been estimated that most adults over 40-years-old display less than 2 per cent of the creative problem-solving ability of a child under 5-years-old.

EXAMPLE – SEEING THE LIGHT

If you place half a dozen bees in a bottle, and the same number of flies, and lie the bottle down horizontally with its base to the window, you will find that the bees will persist, until they die of exhaustion or hunger, in their endeavour to discover a way through the glass. The flies, however, will all have escaped through the neck on the opposite side in less than two minutes.

It is the bees' love of light and their intelligence that is their undoing in this experiment. They evidently imagine that the way out of every prison must be from the direction the light shines. They act in accordance with this assumption and persist in too logical an action. To them, glass is a supernatural mystery they have never met in nature. They have had no experience of this suddenly impenetrable atmosphere. The greater their intelligence, the more inadmissible and incomprehensible the strange obstacle appears.

The flies, on the other hand, are as careless of logic as they are of the enigma of glass. As a result, they disregard the call of the light and simply flutter wildly, hither and thither, until they have the good fortune to discover the opening that restores their liberty.

This example identifies a paradox inherent in learning to solve problems creatively. On the one hand, more education and experience may inhibit creative problem-solving and reinforce conceptual blocks. Like the bees in the story, individuals may not find solutions, because the problem requires less educated, more playful approaches. Influential leaders generate this kind of problem-solving flexibility.

GUIDELINES FOR SUCCESSFUL REFRAMING

1. Practise lifelong learning

Learn from a wide variety of sources. If the reframing is to make sense, it needs to be relevant for the other person. This means that you need to listen and to really hear their point of view. You also need to be able to draw from a variety of sources in order to be flexible and skilled in the way you reframe things for them.

In order to do this, read outside of your normal interests, watch and listen to a range of different news channels, and check out some foreign movies. Learn a little about other people's professions, and, even if you're not a big sports fan, brush up on the basics of different games. Learn about what each major religion provides as a strength or meaning for those who follow that doctrine.

Learning about other people's worldviews becomes even more important if we accept that everyone is unique. Recognising people's uniqueness means knowing that matching and reframing need to be tailored to the individual.

This is because every single person you meet will understand you in their own way as a result of their experiences.

2. Think in analogies

It is helpful to have a wide number of ways that you can describe different situations. This enables you to choose the description that will help the other person reframe their views. An example would be: 'Life is like a box of chocolates; you never know what you are going to get.'

3. Generate alternative interpretations

Consider a number of different ways you might interpret a situation or belief:
- Think about your current interpretation of the person's behaviour/issue.
- Think of a number of alternative interpretations of the same behaviour/issue.
- Pick the one interpretation that seems most plausible and most closely fits their way of acting and thinking.
- Formulate a sentence in your mind that describes the new interpretation.
- Tell them your thoughts.
  Their reaction will let you know whether your reframing fitted or not. A good fit will bring a visible change.

A good way to approach thinking about alternative interpretations of someone's behaviour is to imagine what might have happened to them earlier that day, that week, that month, that year, or even many years ago – and what might be happening to them later that day, that week, that month, or that year.

Did they jump the supermarket queue because they are rude and inconsiderate? Or did they jump the queue because they have just suffered a bereavement, and simply didn't notice you were waiting in line?

Did they pull a face when you made a suggestion in the morning meeting because they thought your idea was terrible, or because they have back pain?

Were they staring at you as you struggled to parallel park because they were judging your driving skills, or was it because you remind them of their best friend?

There are many different reasons for people's behaviour.

Categorisation helps reduce the clutter in our brains by decreasing the amount of information we have to handle each moment. The downside of categorisation is that our understanding of any situation is always partial – we notice just a tiny bit of reality at each moment.

Any set of objects or thoughts can be classified in many different ways, depending on our purposes. Human beings can be grouped by age, sex, nationality, occupation, language, wealth, height, and so on. These are the perspectives of categories, analogies, metaphors, dialectics, and interpretation. Alternative categorisations are one way to understand reframing.

An example of this would be when Tom Sawyer's Aunt Polly makes him whitewash the fence on a Saturday afternoon, when all the other boys are going swimming. His friend Ben comes by and begins to make fun of him for having to work. However, when Tom's reaction is to say that whitewashing the fence suits him fine, as it's not something he's had the chance to do before, Ben quickly wants to join in, followed by the other boys – some of whom are even willing to pay for the chance to have the experience of whitewashing a fence.

Categorisation begins in childhood, and can shape positive or negative mindsets for years to come. How we learn to categorise governs everything, including how we think about our bodies, our intellect, our bravery, our honesty, our ability to lead, our ability to follow, our sense of self-worth, our respect for others, and so on.

The good news is that our frames and concepts are always open to change. A good story hooks us onto a different frame for our goals, and, as our goals change, we notice different things. And when our goals change our actions also change.

Reframing can be offered verbally or non-verbally. A matched raising of the eyebrows, silence, an activity, or a photograph can lead a person to change their point of view.

Use this brief compendium of negative to positive ways of reframing to help build your own reframing capacity.

NEGATIVE BEHAVIOUR	Reframed As	POSITIVE BEHAVIOUR
Worrying.		Focused attention.
Bossy.		Likes to set goals.
Quiet.		Taking care of yourself.
Irritable.		Sensitive to others.
Passive.		Quiet.
Aggressive.		Definite.
Uncertain.		Considers all alternatives.
Defensive.		Protecting yourself.
Too soft.		Caring.
Too hard.		Determined.
Driven.		Keen.
Micromanager.		Wants to understand the details.
Mistakes.		Increased understanding.
Perfection.		Pride in your work.

Many labels are often rooted in our inaccurate perceptions of what is, in fact, normal behaviour. This results from our communication styles. For example, a Gradual person may see a Rapid person as impulsive or error-prone.

INDIRECT WAYS OF REFRAMING

Reframing shows us that indirect communication is far more influencing than direct communication. Indirection doesn't limit our field of view. It is hard to repudiate or resist when the ideas or symbols can never be pinned down. Being indirect means you do not appear to be telling someone what to do or think, and yet you are still conveying the same message to them. Indirect suggestions are a wonderful way of giving the 'illusion of choice', or of having people create their own suggestions as you allow them to put their own interpretation on what you tell them. In this way, they own the idea, not you.

Consider these direct and indirect statements:

'You don't need to get angry!' versus 'I feel as though you may be reacting to what I said.'

'Your project is a waste of time.' versus 'Do you think this project is working in the way you would like?'

'I want you to take on a new manager.' versus 'There are probably several options we can consider to reduce the pressure of work.'

'Do this.' versus 'This is what I have in mind for you, can you suggest anything better?'

The direct statements may seem easier, as they offer a binary choice. The indirect statements are more thoughtful and collaborative, and allow for creative change.

HOW TO USE INDIRECT LANGUAGE

1. Presuppositions

When you've incorporated indirect language into your leadership approach, you will be surprised at just how effective it is.

With this sentence I am 'presupposing' that you *will* incorporate indirect language into your leadership approach.

2. Permissiveness

Making your message permissive is one of the easiest ways to begin making indirect suggestions. Use qualifiers like 'may', 'might', 'could', 'can', and 'perhaps'. For example, a direct suggestion of, 'Stop arguing with Mary.' could be made permissive in various different ways:

'Are there other ways you could encourage Mary to change her position on that?'

'Perhaps Mary doesn't realise how important this matter is.'

'Maybe Mary will respond more positively if you ask her what she wants?'

3. Embedded commands

'It's interesting how without thinking about it at all you will probably make a great presentation today. In this sentence, 'Make a great presentation' is an embedded but hidden direction.

4. Linking

It's easy to learn to use indirect language because you're already reading this section of the book. As you continue to read, you're more likely to go ahead and incorporate the language patterns into your work. The linking word 'because', bypasses the critical 'reason-seeking' that may ordinarily occur without a 'because'/reason. This 'because' theory has been scientifically proven to work. If a person cuts into a queue, there are complaints and objections. However, if the person gives a reason, it is acceptable. The experimenters found that it didn't have to be a good reason – any reason worked, even if it was just, 'because.'

5. Negatives

This is the 'Don't think of a green giraffe' trick.

'I don't want you to think about how well you will do in our meeting tomorrow till you go home tonight.'

6. Imagination

Enabling a colleague to use their imagination to connect to an idea or outcome is very effective.

An example of this is 'future pacing'. Having the person see themselves in the future, succeeding, and overcoming potential challenges, is a strong method of indirect suggestion.

'After you make another brilliant presentation, are you going to take the boss out for a drink?'

STORYTELLING

Stories, using metaphors, similes, and analogies, engage the imagination and are a great way to bypass any critical thinking. This is because you're just listening to a story, not being told what to do or what to think.

A metaphor is a process of reframing. A metaphor is a figure of speech that directly refers to one thing by mentioning another. It may provide (or obscure) clarity or identify hidden similarities between two ideas. All similes and analogies serve a comparable function, by comparing one thing with another.

The story, or relabelling, suggests a different way of looking at the same thing. Stories are popular as they do all the hard lifting for us. A good metaphor distils all the facts into a simple parable, which is what our brain is looking for.

One of the most commonly cited metaphors in English literature comes from As You Like It: 'All the world's a stage, And all the men and women merely players; They have their exits and their entrances.'

Metaphors abound and many become clichés.

'Last one in is a rotten egg.'

'Birds of a feather stick together.'

'The fruit never falls far from the tree.'

'The devil is in the detail.'

The use of metaphors and analogies are a valuable tool in analysing the often complex, ambiguous and paradoxical nature of organisations. Here are some hints that might be helpful when constructing stories:

1. Include action or motion in the analogy. For example, driving a car, cooking a meal, attending a funeral.

2. Include things that can be visualised or pictured in the analogy. For example, stars, football games, crowded shopping malls.

3. Pick familiar events or situations. For example, meetings, presentations, celebrations.

4. Try to relate things that are not obviously similar. For example, saying an organisation is like a crowd is not nearly so rich a simile as saying an organisation is like a children's sandbox or a poker game.

Metaphorical thinking is essential to how we communicate, learn, discover, and invent, and is rooted in pattern-recognition. One simple way to understand this is to think of how we use terms such as 'warm', 'cold', 'bitter', and 'sweet,' literally – to describe physical sensations, and in the abstract – to describe human temperament and personality.

In the same vein, 'I am feeling down' is a metaphor for feeling depressed, whilst, 'I'm high' is a way of saying you're happy. These are similar, familiar, patterns we can easily recognise. A skilful metaphor builds understanding and change.

CASE STUDY – USING EFFECTIVE METAPHORS

Here is a great metaphor from the founder of the NeuroTech Institute, Fiona Kerr, which I will borrow for this example.

A CEO with whom she was working was noted for her excellent empathic leadership skills. However, the 360 feedback consistently revealed her managers' experienced being overlooked by the CEO. Fiona arranged a debriefing session with the CEO to discuss this puzzle. The CEO made great eye contact, was warm, listened attentively, and matched Fiona's body language. Fiona finally hit upon the problem, and created a metaphor to explain it constructively.

She said to the CEO, 'You're a lighthouse.'

'A lighthouse?' the CEO queried.

'Yes,' Fiona continued. 'When you are with a manager, they get your full attention and everything concentrated on them. It's great, and lights them up. Then suddenly the light moves on to another person and they are left completely in the dark.' The CEO resisted this idea and refused to consider it.

The next day she caught up with Fiona and said she shared Fiona's idea with her partner who confirmed the lighthouse metaphor was true!

The CEO then started discussing how she could shine her light in a more encompassing way and make the 'on/off' switch a little less abrupt.

This example illustrates several valuable things: it takes work to change minds; we are often helped by others when we are brave enough to share; and images are powerful.

Pragmatically, nothing prevents you from attempting such metaphors or thoughts yourself. Your brain loves building and exploring structures, concepts, frames, and representations. These constructs then inform and influence perceptions, thinking, and behaviour.

Using stories and metaphors to help people reframe their views helps to reduce friction. It creates ways that the new behaviour can be seen as equal to the old behaviour in terms of perceived risk, benefits, and effort.

HUMOUR AND REFRAMING

Reframing plays an important role in humour, and vice versa. Cartoons, jokes, and caricatures reframe many serious realities. Humour, used effectively, is communication that provides inspiration and offers possibilities. Reframing in general, and humour in particular, builds genuine, memorable connections with others. It shows an enthusiasm and understanding of the other person's needs, while respecting your own.

Children learn about the world through play. As we get to be adults, we spend less time learning in this way. However, we remember things more easily than when they are fun than when they are serious.

Seriousness is attractive to senior leaders as it seems to represent maturity. In fact, seriousness inhibits growth rather than supporting it. Seriousness is rigid and one-dimensional. It can easily make your mindset the only correct one and demands that others enrol.

Maturity, in contrast, means taking responsibility for yourself. Maturity is open-minded, and is not black and white. It allows you to have fun, be wrong, and feel comfortable with that. Maturity provides an internal locus of control with principles and values that are applied flexibly. Learning, changing, and adjusting are fun pursuits. All decisions are viewed as personal choices, and are equally okay.

Seriousness squashes the air out of the devil's advocates, satirists, and cynics in the workplace. However, these people are worth listening to, as there can be a lot of value in what they say. A good leader will note these people are actually committed, even if they are not blindly loyal. Their perspective matters because they present a different frame. Enabling them, rather than merely tolerating, them allows clever leaders to reframe their opposition as a choice.

For leaders, having fun is cautioned because it isn't seen as being appropriate. In some difficult scenarios it is seen as unacceptable, and not in keeping with the importance of the situation. However, using humour astutely is a great way of reframing.

EXAMPLE – USING HUMOUR EFFECTIVELY

Our company was contracted by the Australian Department of Foreign Affairs to work with the leaders of the Personnel Department of the Communist Party of China. Before our first visit, we were given numerous serious lectures on how to behave, which included strict instructions not to use humour. We were told the Chinese people wouldn't understand, and would be offended.

However, we still chose to include humour and cartoons in our presentations on performance, leadership, and change. Rather than causing offence, our training rooms were filled with laughter and learning.

EXAMPLES OF REFRAMING

These examples are about another person's comments, but you can also use the guidelines to shift your own perspectives.

1. Shift from passive to active

Colleague: 'I just can't do anything about this.'

Response: 'What is the first step you might take if you did start on it?'

2. Shift from past to future

Colleague: 'I've never been any good at handling confrontation.'

Response: 'If you imagined you were good at it, what might you say to Fred?'

3. Shift from future to pas

Colleague: 'I can't get started on achieving this goal.'

Response: 'Hey, sometime in the past when you achieved a goal, what did you do back then to be successful? How might you use that approach now?'

4. Shift from others to oneself

Colleague: 'My team don't seem to trust me.'

Response: 'What do you value about yourself?'

5. Shift from a liability to an asset

Colleague: 'I always overdo it. I'm such a perfectionist.'

Response: 'How might being a perfectionist help in this project though?'

6. Shift from victimisation to empowerment

Colleague: 'That always seems to happen to me.'

Response: 'Sometimes we even do that to ourselves. Perhaps it'd be useful to explore if you're somehow doing that to yourself, too?'

EXERCISE – REFRAMING

Spend a little time thinking of other examples of reframing that you have used, or upcoming situations where you might employ reframing:

....
....
....
....
....
....
....
....
....
....
....
....
....
....
....
....
....
....
....

Reframing requires you to step back from what is being said and done and to consider the frame, or 'lens' through which the reality is being created.

You need to take the time to look at the situation from the outside. This enables you to understand the unspoken assumptions, including beliefs and schema that are being used, and to pay attention to the body language and voice tone. Even if it is a tense situation – especially if it is a tense situation – pause and get in touch with your prefrontal cortex.

Influential leadership could be simply expressed as 'pause before you speak'.

While reflecting, consider, create, and imagine alternative lenses so that you can look at the situation in another way.

Challenge the beliefs or other aspects of the frame. Ask yourself why you believe it. Consider where the idea came from. Look at how A and B connect in your approach to the situation.

Stand in another frame and describe what you see. Ask yourself what the situation might look like from the union's point of view. Think about what your team would say if they were there. Run through what your partner might think about the idea.

Change attributes of the frame to reverse the meaning. Select and ignore some words and actions to emphasise or downplay various elements. For example:

Colleague: 'If Mark stays on the project it will never finish on time and I won't be held responsible for the mess with the client.'

Response: 'I'll handle the client, so how can I help you get the timelines and schedule working well?' This ignores the complaint and assumes Mark is staying on the project.

In this way, you can reframe:

- Problems as opportunities.
- Weaknesses as strengths.
- Impossibilities as distant possibilities.
- Distant possibilities as near possibilities.
- Oppression (against me) as neutral (doesn't care about me).
- Unkindness as lack of understanding.

You can often change a person's frame by changing their emotional state, encouraging them to be happier, more forthright, and so on. When they are happier they will be more positive and optimistic. For example:

'You say it can't be done in time. But what if we staged delivery or got in extra help? I'm sure we can produce an acceptable product in the time frame'.

'It does seem stupid, but it's also stupid not to look again and see what else can be done.'

'It's not so much doing away with old ways, as building a new and more effective future.'

'We have shown we can argue well. Maybe this means we can also agree well.'

TWO ILLUSTRATIONS OF REFRAMING

1. The Nine Dot Puzzle

Draw four lines connecting all the dots, without lifting the pen from the page.

The Nine Dot Puzzle

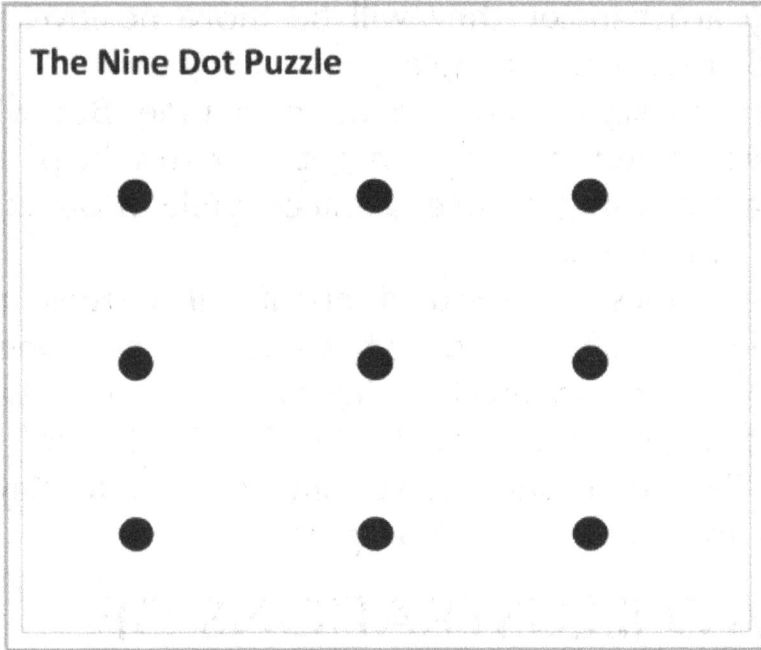

*The solution is see section entitled "REVIEW YOUR INFLUENCE-SUPPORTING SKILLS"

2. The Flour Puzzle

This second example is taken from J. Barton Cunningham's book, *Researching Organizational Values and Beliefs: The Echo Approach.*[15]

'A woman was once kneading dough in front of the centre pole of her tent. She needed more flour. Since the bag of flour was behind the pole, she bent down, encircling the pole with her arms as she cupped her hands, and scooped out some flour from the bag. When she tried to get the flour to the dough that she had been kneading, she found that the tent pole obstructed her cupped hands. She did not want to drop the flour back into the bag for fear of wasting it. Not knowing what to do, she began to cry. A Mullah came along, and he gave her a suggestion that solved the problem. What did he suggest? The Mullah had told the lady to walk around the tent pole until her cupped hands were directly over the dough she had been kneading, and then to drop the flour on the dough.'

Both of these examples illustrate a creative, thinking outside the square aspect to reframing. Only after you have reframed the problem does it appear obvious. You wonder why you didn't see it at once.

Everything is a viewpoint, and there is no neutral position.

Think about how important music is in film. It can change the same collection of events in any movie from a comedy into a horror show. The way we frame past events and current events is much like a soundtrack in film.

Framing can make us successful at getting what we want, or unsuccessful. Success means knowing the other person's soundtrack and insinuating our music with theirs. You both tune in to the same tune. Your mindset shapes how you frame your music. A jangled, unfocused mindset produces a discordant tune. A clear strong mindset produces a purposeful, inspiring tune.

We have been learning how to change the music we produce to be more harmonious, by using our prefrontal cortex. That's part of consciousness, and that's what positive framing wrestles with – evaluating the situation rationally and considering alternatives that promote a more measured response.

That is positive reframing.

Both positive framing and negative framing are equally true. But by taking a matching approach, we provide a perspective that is more easily absorbed by the other person.

Recent evidence discovered in clinical trials conducted in the Netherlands suggests that physical activity can be more effectively promoted to older adults with positive messages about the benefits of activity rather than with negative messages about the risks of inactivity. Older adults who received positively framed messages about the benefits of physical activity increased their exercise engagement significantly over their peers who received negatively framed messages about the risks of failing to exercise more.

Studies have also shown that negative framing will generate unnecessary anticipatory anxiety. Positive framing reduces stress, which inhibits the attention directed toward the seemingly adverse event or condition.

Reframing is often achieved through visualisation, where people are asked to visualise a new outcome before they engage in a task.

CASE STUDY – VISUALISATION

College students were divided into two groups. One group was asked to visualise themselves looking at a board where their grades on a final exam would be posted, and to visualise an 'A' grade by their name. This procedure was repeated several times before the exam.

The other group was asked to create a different mental simulation. They were asked to imagine the process of studying for the exam. They were told to imagine all the steps, ways, and places where they would study for the exam. This group visualised the process of studying, where the first group visualised the outcome.

The group who imagined themselves studying outperformed the group visualising their grade.

We know the mind becomes primed to follow through on the things we visualise. This case study demonstrates that visualising an action leads to following through on that action, and it's our actions that get results.

So reframing needs to focus on our actions, and is helped by visualising 'choice points'. Choice points are the moments in time when your actions will either lead you *towards* your goal or *away* from it. Visualise the actions you will take to make your desired goal a reality. Don't visualise the outcome. Instead, visualise the path you need to take that will lead you to your goal.

POSITIVE AND NEGATIVE FRAMING

You can view anything from at least two different frames, and both frames can be true. Positive framing just happens to be healthier. Positive framing does not produce the same fear as negative framing.

Negative framing

- Slows down brain coordination.
- Makes it difficult to process thoughts and find solutions.
- Hinders creative ability.
- Decreases activity in the cerebellum.
- Impacts the Amygdala (fear factor), affecting mood, memory, and impulse control.

Positive framing

- Synapses (areas connecting neurons) increase dynamically.
- Increases mental productivity by improving cognition.
- Intensifies ability to pay attention, to focus.

- Improves ability to think and analyse incoming data.
- Improves ability to solve problems quicker and enhance creativity.

Some of these aspects of framing are expanded upon in Daniel Goleman's book *Focus: The Hidden Driver of Excellence*.[16]

But what about your internal conversations? In the course of the day, your consciousness flicks through thousands of past, current, and future events and circumstances. You can reframe some of those descriptors by changing your tune. You can literally rewrite your own history.

Shit happens. Sometimes you just need to live with it – you can't find a parking place and you are late for an important meeting. Other times things aren't as bad as you thought they would be – you can't find a parking place, but the meeting starts late. Sometimes what seemed shitty at the time turns out to be a positive – the car in the parking place you missed out on had a wall collapse on it.

In the same way as you can reframe what is happening in the world around you, it is possible to reframe your self-image.

For example, reframe your anxiety as excitement. This will enable you to share your ideas with others. Physiologically, anxiety and excitement share the same brain location. By the same token, reframe asking for help as collaborating with your teams and creating an inclusive environment, rather than seeing it as a sign of weakness or incompetence.

Framing is not about what is fact. It's about how those facts are perceived. Positive framing allows you to move forward – it's about gain. Negative framing often stops you in your tracks—it's about loss.

At a functional level, being focused on negative thoughts slows down brain processing speeds. This is why it's harder to put your thoughts together when you are upset, and harder to find a positive solution to a problem.

Through poor framing, a negative outlook might very well become your negative outcome. The challenge is this – how often can we positively frame or reframe events we instinctually frame negatively?

Consider that your hidden thoughts can reveal themselves in many ways.

EXAMPLES – FRAMING

Thought
'I don't want to hurt his feelings'.
Reframed thought
'What could he learn and develop from this matter?'
Thought
'I was wrong and feel bad about what I did/said.'
Reframed thought

'How can I give an example so my apology is more convincing?'

Thought

'They are so nasty/dumb/painful/wrong'.

Reframed thought

'What is the evidence? Why do I believe this? Could I be mistaken? Might I have a possible bias or negative impression that is about my feelings and not their character?'

Thought

'They never appreciate me/understand me/value me'.

Reframed thought

'What might I be doing to contribute to that view? How can I share my thoughts to encourage different behaviour?'

Thought

'Why can't they just do what they're told/perform properly/deliver on time/grow up?'

Reframed thought

'What do I need to do to assist them to perform properly/deliver on time?'

FIRST AND SECOND ORDER CHANGE

Reframing is akin to the concept of second order change.

First order change is where you have a problem and throw a solution at it. If that doesn't work, you escalate and try a stronger solution. And so on.

First order change works within an existing structure and view of the world. You might see it as tinkering with the system – doing more or less of something, making an existing process better or more accurate, and making incremental changes.

With first order change, the ends of the system remain the same – it's the means of producing those results that change. What you seek, what you avoid, the way you see the world, and your values remain the same. It is safe leadership.

From an organisational perspective, one problem with first order change is that any given way of seeing the world does not usually serve the interests of all the organisation's members equally. It is often here and now, tunnel-vision thinking, and short-term leadership.

Second order change is a reframe. It switches the focus from the problem to the solutions. You reconsider previous failed solutions and look for some 'out of the box' ideas about what is wrong with that solution. You brainstorm a host of wildly different options. It is paradoxical, and disrupts common sense.

Second order change is often described as 'transformational', 'paradoxical, or 'disruptive'. It involves the leader actually seeing the world in a different way, challenging assumptions, and working from a new and different worldview or frame of reference. Recall the nine dot puzzle.

Inevitably, second order change involves new ways of doing things, changing values and goals, and probably structural change in the organisation as well. This can be quite scary to most people, especially where changes are imposed from above or outside, and you don't have any input to them.

CASE STUDY – SECOND ORDER CHANGE

An executive was speaking to me about one of their managers who had an increasingly bad drinking problem. They had tried several interventions, all of which had failed. They had expressed sympathy and tried to help the manager, and when that didn't work, they said that the manager's behaviour was affecting others in the team. When that didn't work, they put him on a performance improvement plan to end the drinking at work. That escalation didn't work either, and they began to have discussions with the manager about termination.

In our discussion we explored a whole range of options. The executive went off to consider these, and in the next session reported back what had happened. They had decided to promote him!

The executive put the manager in an important position with some team members who were needing some help and would rely on the manager considerably. It was clearly a very responsible, important part of the organisation. This was truly a paradoxical solution. And it worked. The manager sobered up, joined AA, and put in significant effort.

The manager later told the executive that they felt useless before, and believed that no one respected them. The promotion was the first expression of trust the manager had received, and they didn't want to let the executive down.

GRATITUDE

The basic virtue of gratitude is also a feature of reframing and influential leadership.

The 'glass half empty' leaders see what they have not achieved and feel miserable, while the 'glass half full' leaders see what they have gained and are grateful.

You can reframe your past, your present, and your future. You can reimagine your past, be flexible in the present, and develop a positive expectancy about the future.

A good way to think about gratitude is to imagine you're shovelling a pile of sand, and to remember to have a look behind you at how much sand you have shifted.

BIAS

Biases are the internal negative framings of life. We are all biased. The biggest bias we all have is thinking we are unbiased.

We often use this exercise with our seminar groups to illustrate how bias works.

We put forward the statement that an open bottle of tomato sauce must be kept in the fridge.

We then ask those people who agree with this statement to raise their hands.

In every group about half of the participants put their hands up. We then ask the fridge people to pair up with the non-fridge people and try to convince the other person why they are wrong.

The bottom line is that there is absolutely no compelling data to support the statement that tomato sauce must be stored in the fridge. Factual arguments don't change the other person's view. It is simply a personal preference, which becomes a belief, which becomes a bias, which becomes a truth.

Now a tomato sauce bottle is just a minor bias, so consider how more serious biases might have a significant impact on leadership. Thinking about mismatched ID dimensions, it is a common unconscious judgement for a Rapid person to misperceive a Gradual person as being 'slow' or even 'dumb'. Similarly, an Understater can feel that an Exaggerator is trying to con them.

Either bias might possibly be true, but it needs to be verified rather than being assumed. This is the whole point of the reactive, generalising primitive brain versus the careful analysis of the prefrontal cortex.

Being aware of potential biases before the conversation even starts brings our bias into focus, rather than it shaping our conversation through unawareness. Our conscious and unconscious biases and assumptions are embedded in our body, and subtly impact our attitude and non-verbal behaviour.

These are still small biases in comparison to biases such as, 'Go back to where you came from,' 'Trump is a great leader,' 'Climate change is a hoax,' 'Greenies are great,' 'There is no God,' and so on. These big biases are usually deal breakers, so we are concentrating on the less extreme biases to help you be successful.

In terms of leadership, the important thing to remember is that each unmanaged bias conveys evidence of why you are possibly unreliable, untrustworthy, and unlikely to be effective.

An important cognitive bias to be aware of is the **transparency bias.** This bias causes us to overestimate how obvious our inner world is to others. We think that what we're saying, feeling, and thinking is absolutely clear to other people. Often, it isn't that evident.

We underestimate how explicit our communication needs to be, and so we are not at all clear. With this bias we may come across as irritable and impatient with the other person's stupidity.

Another bias that can easily impact leadership is the **attribution bias.** The 'fundamental attribution error' is our bias to judge other people differently from how we judge ourselves. It is described as, 'the tendency to believe that what people do reflects who they are'—for better and for worse.

EXAMPLE – THE ATTRIBUTION BIAS

When I interrupt someone during a meeting it is because I want to help, and I am being considerate.

When someone else interrupts me during a meeting it is because they are being rude and inconsiderate.

As a leader, if you continually interrupt others during meetings, but express annoyance if anyone interrupts you, then you are likely to be viewed as having double standards, or thinking your ideas are better than anyone else in room.

Another example of this is the way we can take credit for the good stuff that happens and blame the bad stuff on luck, so that it won't be our fault. The leadership result is that we don't learn and develop.

Another very common bias is the **confirmation bias,** which is when we seek out and interpret data in a way that strengthens our pre-established opinions. For example, Fred only watches Fox News and Amra only views SBS. When world events happen, their bias is confirmed by their selected media.

Another example would be that if I believe you are resistant to my ideas, and when we are talking you frown and change the topic, I interpret these signs as confirmation of my bias. In fact, you may be fascinated, concentrating, and reflecting. So when I say, 'Well I can see you don't agree!' you will feel perplexed and blocked out.

When we present people with information that contradicts their opinion, this can cause them to come up with altogether new counter-arguments that further strengthen their original view. This is known as the 'boomerang effect'.

One further bias that is very relevant to leadership is the **framing effect bias.** We don't make choices in isolation. We are highly dependent on the way things are presented to us. For example, a big meal on a small plate is more fulfilling than a small meal on a big plate. We tend to fall prey to framing on a daily basis.

You're more likely to buy a 'special deal' pen for five dollars if you previously saw another pen that cost twenty dollars. Even though the price of the more expensive pen is irrelevant to your buying decision, the cognitive bias of framing will lead you to perceive the lower priced pen as a cheap bargain, even though it may not be.

EXAMPLE – FRAMING EFFECT BIAS

I was having a leadership session with a CEO recently whose effectiveness was greatly diminished by his fear of flying. Often, he cancelled international flights at the last minute as his fear became overwhelming.

As well as working with the CEO, I had been working extensively with his executive team for several months. Having gone through other leadership skills with him he finally felt safe enough to say that he needed help with his flight phobia, and that he wanted to fix it before his team found out about it.

I said, 'It's too late, they already know!'

He and I laughed. It threw the 'hidden phobia' into a whole new light. He was more upset about being exposed as weak than being scared of flying. They knew, and still supported him 100 per cent. This reframe enabled an easier solution to be found.

There are some questions you can ask yourself to help unearth any biases in your beliefs or your counterpart's beliefs:

1. Why do I believe this? How do I know it's true?
2. What are other views about this?
3. Why might they be right?

These questions can help us to have good influential conversations when we need to, and to develop and enlarge our leadership skills.

Biases are like gravity. They are invisible, but they influence everything we do and say. Despite arising from the amygdala, biases are not hard wired. They can be unlearned. Being aware of our biases and modifying them is essential to us getting what we want. It is important to address these as comprehensively as possible. Our bias also picks away at our big assumptions.

REFRAMING SKILLS SUMMARY

- Be aware of how you filter and shape what you see and hear.
- Examine your biases and prejudices, and reduce or remove them.
- Say what you want directly in your head, then say it differently.
- Listen to what the other person says and say it back with a slight twist.
- Compose stories.
- Take a specific negative and turn it into a specific positive.
- Build your expectant attitude.

8

OBSERVING

'Ah, Watson, you see but you do not observe.'

– Sherlock Holmes

OBSERVING AND UNDERSTANDING

Most effective influence occurs when you accurately understand what influences your counterpart. Knowing what drives them is your signal for what you need to do to influence them. Knowing depends on observing.

Observing your own communication

How well do you observe your own communication style? Awareness of your skill and style of communication is a major feature of understanding yourself and being understood by others.

Communication, both verbal and non-verbal, is the foundation of understanding. Yet we so easily take it for granted. Communicating so that we are influential is a very individual and complex skill.

COMMUNICATION QUIZ

Answer the following questions using this score key:

Score Key

1. None of the time.
2. Some of the time.
3. A lot of the time.
4. All the time.

Questions

1. I watch people closely when I talk with them.

2. I put a lot of energy into my communication.

3. I think about the best way to make myself understood.

4. I pay attention to the speed of the person's communication.

5. I get a sense of the other person before raising my proposition.

6. I use some of the way they see the world in my communication with them.

7. I plan what I want to say before my meeting.

8. I plan the way I want to present my communication before the meeting.

9. I consciously adjust my presentation style according to the nature of the other person's communication.

10. I am comfortable with silence during my discussions.

11. I feel good about myself when I am talking with others.

12. I attempt to give the other person a sense of their worth when I talk to them.

13. I am curious about the other person's presentation.

14. I am patient in my communication.

15. Later on, I reflect positively on my communications.

TOTAL SCORE: _____

If you scored 50 to 60—You are a master communicator.

If you scored 40 to 50—You are a good communicator.

If you scored 30 to 40—Your communication will benefit from some practice and careful planning.

If you scored 15 to 30—You need to improve your communication skills.

Observing respectfully is one of the most basic skills of great leadership. It is so very simple, yet we rarely do it well, if at all. The more you see, the more you know. The more you know, the more you understand. The more you understand, the more influential you will be.

Observing a person while we are speaking with them has become a lost art. We rehearse what we will say next. We are distracted by other things. We are easily embarrassed. We don't want to reveal too much of ourselves. So we don't observe very closely at all.

Observing demonstrates two things. First, it shows you are truly *interested* in the other person. Second, it helps you learn about their way of being, and whether your communication is connecting. It shows you their perspective and frame of reference.

People are lazy. It takes less energy to pulse cooperatively than to pulse in opposition. Physicists call this beautiful economical laziness 'mutual phase locking' or 'entrainment'. All living beings are oscillators. We vibrate. We pulse. We move rhythmically and change rhythmically. We keep time.

Like the two pendula, through more complex processes, two people can mutually phase-lock. Successful human relationship involves entrainment, or 'getting in sync'. This is mirroring. If we aren't in sync, the relationship is either uncomfortable or problematic.

The most fundamental of all human needs is the need to be taken seriously. Everything else flows from that. So it's no wonder good listeners are so highly prized, and so good at achieving their goals.

Listening with your focus on the person speaking shows that you are taking them seriously. Observing them closely takes them seriously. Speaking in a matched, connected way takes them seriously.

Facts are solid and testable. Interpretation is what you do with facts. It is how you perceive the facts through your biases and values. You then have an emotional reaction based on your interpretation of the facts. Your emotional reaction generally causes you to pursue some end.

To be more effective, set aside your interpretations, reactions and ends, and start processing and reflecting on the facts.

LADDER OF INFERENCE

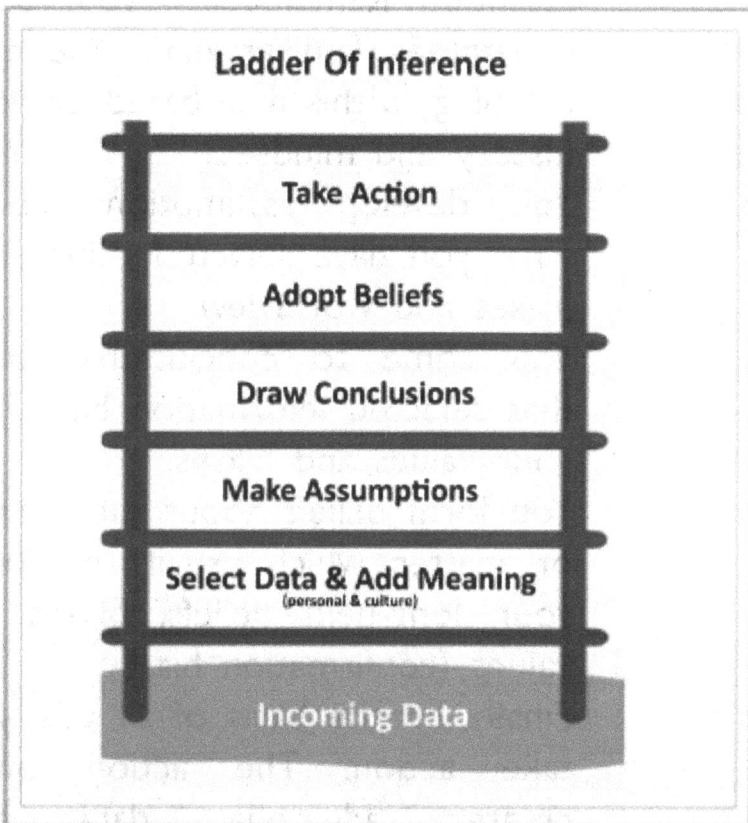

Ladder Of Inference

Take Action

Adopt Beliefs

Draw Conclusions

Make Assumptions

Select Data & Add Meaning
(personal & culture)

Incoming Data

This ladder is adapted from Peter Senge's brilliant concept.[17]

Let's start at the bottom with all the data the hits you – the facts of what you actually observe or experience. It rapidly progresses to the top level of actions.

Step 1.   You see, hear, and feel some factual event or communication.

Step 2.   You then (physiologically and psychologically) unconsciously select only some of that data and experience to which you pay attention. Remember – your brain generalises familiar data. You affix meaning to this data based on your history and mindset.

Step 3.   You develop assumptions about what you have selected using your biases and worldview.

Step 4.   You come to conclusions about that selected information based on your values and biases.

Step 5.   You form beliefs about the person or matter, which usually reinforce your long-held beliefs, biases, or values (confirmation bias).

Step 6.   Finally, on the basis of all this, you take action. The action often creates additional data and experiences, which takes you straight to the bottom of the next ladder.

EXAMPLE – LADDER OF INFERENCE

Jane is conducting a team meeting and she notices Kim and his behaviour (real data and experience).

She observes that Kim is frowning and looking away on several occasions (selected data).

She fails to observe his suit, or that he is taking notes and deep in concentration. From the narrow bit of selected data she has selected, she thinks that because he is frowning and looking away this means he is not interested in what she is saying (affixed meaning).

She assumes that he is doing this because he doesn't agree with her point of view (assumption).

She then concludes that he doesn't support her as the manager of the team (conclusions).

This reinforces her belief that he wanted her job himself (belief).

As a result, she decides to manage his performance more closely (action).

This sequence, of course, virtually ensures that the outcome Jane imagined becomes a reality, even if, in fact, Kim was preoccupied with his relationship break-up and trying hard as hard as he could to focus on the meeting.

All these steps on the ladder can happen in a few minutes and can really interfere with Jane's leadership by causing considerable stress and conflict.

So how do we avoid the ladder?

Obviously you can't go through life without making some assumptions, generalising from experience, adding meaning, or drawing conclusions. It would be very inefficient and cumbersome, not to mention boring.

However, you can improve your communication and effectiveness through careful understanding of the nature of the ladder of inference. Especially in those really important conversations.

Here are some suggestions:

- Increase your level of self-awareness.
- Do not assume you are right.
- Identify some of your pet assumptions and beliefs and develop an early warning signal if they are triggered.
- Whenever you make a negative assumption or conclusion, make your thinking transparent to the other person and check out your perceptions with them.
- Ask others, 'How did this incident occur? Let's review how we got to this point'.

- Employ the 'I see, I imagine, and I feel' technique.

In the example above, Jane could stop and say, 'Kim, I notice that you are frowning, and I wonder if there is any difficulty?' Alternatively, she could ask Kim if he agrees with what she is saying. Finally, she could have a private conversation with Kim after the meeting, share her impressions, and ask him for his perceptions of the meeting.

TIPS FOR ACTIVE LISTENING

1. Restate what you heard – to make sure you understand and to show that you are paying attention.

2. Ask questions – to encourage the other person to elaborate on their thoughts and feelings. Avoid jumping to conclusions about what they mean.

3. Match body language – show that you are interested by making eye contact, nodding, facing the other person, and maintaining an open and relaxed body posture.

4. Avoid labelling the person and their point of view – focus on understanding the other person's perspective and accepting it for what it is, even if you disagree with it.

5. Take turns to speak – by first engaging in these active listening steps and then asking if it's okay for you to share your perspective. By the way don't just listen to them, listen to yourself.

THE DRAMA TRIANGLE

This triangle has been adapted from Karpman's Drama Triangle.[18]

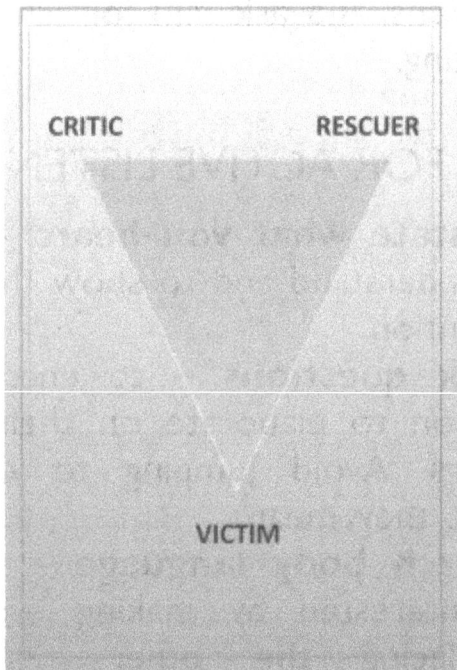

The three positions of Critic, Rescuer, and Victim are roles or stances we adopt from our old assumptions. They are roles we take on when we feel stressed. They all occur when our inadequacy pops to the surface. We feel vulnerable and exposed so we rescue, criticise or take on the role of the victim.

Playing in the drama triangle is confirmation we are not being responsible and accountable. The root of much unhappiness at work (and elsewhere) is an unwillingness to take responsibility for one's life.

These three roles are not descriptions of who you are. They're descriptions of how you're behaving when you aren't being truly honest with yourself.

As we discussed right back at the beginning, if we take responsibility for our actions, thoughts, and behaviours we cannot enjoy playing in the drama triangle.

Someone starts the triangle from their favourite position, hooks in a responsive player and off we go on a repetitive routine we all recognise. But we only recognise it after it is over.

Then, with the sureness of day and night, we leap into it yet again on another day, with the same person or with a new person. Couples are professional drama triangle players.

Mostly, we are completely unaware of our beliefs and attitudes. We are often unaware of the roles themselves. However, reading through the roles provides a recognition of the fundamental universality of this routine.

Rescuer role

The rescuer role is the helper, enabler, social worker, or mediator – the person who wants to 'fix' the problem. A Rescuer needs a person with a problem. That's your first warning!

The core belief is, 'Don't worry, I will take it on and fix it.' This comes from feeling responsibility for everything.

The problem of rescuing is that it comes from an unconscious need to feel important or to be seen as helpful or necessary. Taking care of others is the best way a Rescuer knows how to connect or feel special.

Very often, Rescuers hope that if they take care of others well enough, they will be recognised and rewarded. Of course this rarely happens. A poor response means they might switch roles and be a Critic – 'After all my advice and support you still did the wrong thing!' or, 'No matter how much I help you, it's never enough.'

Rescuers often try making themselves indispensable and are blind to the dependency they foster. The help they provide is not empowering, nor successful. The Victim is not expected to solve the problem without the Rescuer. The Rescuer sees Victims as unable to cope, unable to do it on their own, and failures. That's your second clue. It's a very popular role in the triangle because we feel so noble – we are helping people! However, it's actually our amygdala in overdrive.

To avoid taking on the rescuer role, notice your need to be helpful. Check your motives.

Are you *really* helping or just wanting to be liked? Only help when asked.

When you feel a superhero urge coming upon you, be aware that you're about to leap into the Rescuer role. The minute you believe the other person needs your help, especially if they have not asked for it, you are in danger of starting the drama triangle. Remind yourself that people are much stronger than they sometimes appear, and they don't need you to confirm they are not coping with this moment. Let them handle it.

Critic role

This is a control role, with a dose of judgement thrown in. The Critic role also needs Victims. This is the first clue.

There is an authoritative negative energy about playing the Critic. Being in charge is very important. Settling scores is often familiar behaviour.

The Critic needs someone to blame. The core belief is, 'I'm surrounded by fools'. What makes it a little confusing is the Critic role often parallels high technical expertise. They often are the most intelligent or most skilled people in the room. They have data and correctness on their side.

When you are in the Critic role you will not succeed in the long term, because you cannot *command* people to give to you. Why are you giving direction, correction, or inspection?

To avoid falling into the critic role, ask yourself if it is *really* that important. Consider what will happen if you keep quiet. Are you concerned about being vulnerable? Why? Be honest with yourself, what is needed to give up a little control?

When you find yourself using phrases like these you are probably embracing the Critic role:

'You're completely wrong,' 'I'm certain', 'Listen here', 'I knew it', 'It always happens this way', 'You don't know what you're talking about', 'That's just not true'. From the influential communication perspective, it closes off discussion and resolution possibilities.

Whenever you're irritated and have the 'finger-pointing blame sensation', you're about to be a Critic. Step back and let it go. Alternatively, identify different approaches or options that you can take to address things without being critical of the other person.

Victim role

Victims play helpless with great dexterity. They do not acknowledge their achievements or their capacity to solve their own problems. Their resilience is low, so they rarely persevere long enough to draw on their usually abundant internal resources. True Victims have obvious reasons for being helpless. They are palpably in shock.

However, there is something contrived about the Victim role. They are not direct – they don't ask for help, they insinuate it.

The core belief is, 'Life is so unfair,' which comes from the understanding that, 'I'm inadequate and can't change.'

The Victim role is a spiral into more helplessness. Often, chronic Victim players don't even need to ask for help. They insinuate that they are not coping, and a Rescuer leaps in.

One little sign of the power they have lies in the tendency of Victims to be passive aggressive. If you've been blindsided by a skilful Victim you will recognise this immediately.

When a person rescues or criticises a Victim they reinforce, confirm, and cement their victimhood. It limits the Victim's chances of learning, growing up, and being successful on their own.

Usually, when you start being a Victim, the matter about which you are feeling hard done by is minor and not serious. Instead of hoping to get looked after, you need to take responsibility.

It is important to remember that you are not a Victim. You get dressed and earn a living. You are capable. You have accomplished things. You do not need help.

We all engage in the triangle. These roles are self-inflicted and self-limiting. Stepping away from the triangle is one of the toughest things to do on the journey to becoming responsible and accountable.

Work on being better at noticing when you're invited to play, and avoid the game – and forgive yourself if you fail. Remember that it is important to respect the other person even if they are addicted to the triangle. This is their way of safeguarding themselves against their assumptions of threat.

The good news...

Hidden behind the problems of these roles are some valuable qualities.

The Rescuer is a person who can be good at facilitating and problem solving. Critics can be good power and inspirational models, and Victims have the capacity to be humble servant leaders.

As a system, this triangle is alive and hopping. We usually learn our primary position of Rescuer, Critic or Victim from our family. This is our 'go to' role. We also rotate through the other positions, skilfully switching roles to keep everyone on their toes. This can occur sometimes in a matter of minutes, many times every week.

The Critic and Rescuer roles are on the upper end of the triangle. From either position we are relating as though we are in a stronger position than the Victim. Sooner or later the Victim builds resentment and switches into the Critic role. Then the Rescuer may become a

Victim and a new routine commences. The Rescuer could also become a Critic for an alternative routine.

Obviously, each position reflects our mindset, as each has its own particular way of seeing and reacting to the world. In the Victim role people see the world as a battlefield where it is hard to keep their head above water. In the Critic role people see the world as, 'My way or no way.' And the Rescuer role is, 'My purpose is to help people.'

As well as playing with other people we can also effortlessly conduct this triangle inside our own heads. Here's an example of typical internal triangle conversations:

Victim: 'I can't do this.'

Rescuer: 'Sure you can, here's how.'

Critic: 'I don't need any bloody help.'

Alternatively...

Critic: 'You didn't stand up for yourself – again!'

Victim: 'I know. I just get so weak and uncertain.'

Rescuer: 'Well you didn't want to hurt her feelings, so it's probably for the best.'

Another way of looking at the drivers of leadership behaviour is through **Transactional Analysis.**

TRANSACTIONAL ANALYSIS

Created by Eric Berne,[19] Transactional Analysis looks at three 'ego states' – parent, adult, and child, which are largely shaped through childhood experiences.

Transactional Analysis is a very practical relationship process, based on the internalised messages we took from our parents. It is a way of describing interactions, either between two adults or inside our own heads. The Drama Triangle is part of that system.

Transactional Analysis works in the following way:

Critical parent/leader: 'Be very careful how you raise that issue in the executive meeting.' This verbal command is accompanied by non-verbal signals such as finger wagging, frowning, and speaking in a loud or abrasive tone of voice.

Rebellious child/colleague: 'I'll raise the issue in the way I consider appropriate.' This verbal response is accompanied by non-verbal signals such as chin-up, clenched fists, and speaking in an aggressive tone of voice.

This exchange leads to:

Critical parent/leader: 'Just remember who you're speaking to!'

Rebellious child/colleague: 'You don't know everything.'

Alternatively...

Nurturing parent/leader: 'That issue needs to be handled sensitively in the executive meeting.' This verbal command is accompanied by non-verbal signals such as smiling and speaking in a quiet and gentle tone of voice.

Compliant child/colleague: 'Yes, absolutely. I'll think about the best way to bring it up.' This verbal command is accompanied by non-verbal signals such as smiling, making eye contact, and speaking in a warm and thoughtful tone of voice.

These two approaches lead to vastly different outcomes.

It may help to consider that all positions on the Drama Triangle are parent/child interactions, and that breaking up the triangle is always an adult/adult transaction.

EXAMPLE – PARENT/CHILD DRAMA TRIANGLE INTERACTION

Adult/Adult exchange.

Boss: 'How's your presentation to the Board coming long?'

Executive team member: 'Great. Thanks for asking.'

Alternatively, the executive team member perceives the boss as the Critical Parent and takes the role of the Compliant Child.

Boss: 'How's your presentation to the Board coming long?'

> Executive team member: 'I'm not sure, it's probably not what you were looking for. I'm sorry, I tried my best.'
>
> *Finally, the executive team member perceives the boss as the Critical Parent and takes the role of the Rebellious Child.*
>
> Boss: 'How's your presentation to the Board coming long?'
>
> Executive team member: 'Why don't you wait and see, before criticising it!'

None of these three roles necessarily mean we are operating selfishly or without caring for other people. Rescuers can genuinely care and be worried about a person in need. Victims can experience frightening hopelessness, and Critics can be doing what they believe is best.

The difference is in the switch:

- If Rescuers don't get the appreciation they feel they deserve, they can shut down.
- If Victims don't get the help and assurance they want, they can become passive aggressive.
- If Critics don't get praised for their input, they can become unkind.

Avoiding The Triangle

1.	Be grown up, be honest with yourself, and take full responsibility.

2.   Spot the triangle from the very first manoeuvre. And simply stop playing.

You know now your favourite role. So be alert to invites from your complementary player and don't play. Be honest with yourself. Remember that Rescuers attract Victims and Critics, Victims attract Rescuers and Critics, and Critics attract Victims and Rescuers.

EXAMPLES – HOW TO AVOID THE TRIANGLE

Scenario One

Victim (sighing deeply): 'The boss was horrible to me today.'

Response: 'What happened?'

Victim: 'He told me off.'

Response: 'What did you say?'

Victim: 'I explained why it had happened, but it didn't seem to make any difference.'

Response: 'That's a pity. What are you going to do now?'

The same scenario in reverse

Rescuer: 'I saw you had a meeting with the boss. It looked a bit rough. How are you feeling?'

Response: 'All okay. Thanks for asking. See you.'

Scenario Two

Critic: 'This report is a right mess. What's up with you?'

Response: 'Can you show me exactly what you want done differently?'

Each of these is an adult/adult reply to the Drama Triangle invitation. Even if you feel angry or guilty or you made a bad mistake, you still play it straight. This is being grown up and responsible. It stops the triangle.

The Victim may feel guilty and want to sign a confession, but they don't.

The Rescuer may want to help but acknowledges internally they are actually helping themselves, rather than the other person.

The Critic often has the hardest challenge. They need to be willing to be more vulnerable.

Be warned – some players are hardcore and will do everything to keep you in the triangle.

The adult responses above will be met with anger, tears, or blaming you for now being a Critic.

Respecting that people may react and take time to see things in a new light means sometimes you just need to walk away, even when it is not all understanding and harmony.

You may need to live with your own discomfort about yourself and the other person. Some benefit derives from the understanding about the dysfunction caused by The Drama Triangle.

Like biases, The Drama Triangle is also an invisible and pervasive routine that insinuates itself into too much of our communication.

Leaders are seduced into The Drama Triangle when their amygdala triumphs over their prefrontal cortex. It most often sucks us in when there is a workplace conflict between two or more staff.

Inevitably, we go for The Drama Triangle when we decide that the conflict is due to a personality clash.

Personality clash is only one of four sources of workplace conflict. The other three are **role incompatibility, poor communication systems,** and **workplace stress.**

Each source requires a different approach. Attributing conflict to a personality clash, when it's actually one of the other three causes, is very untidy.

A leader whose prefrontal cortex holds the amygdala in check doesn't make this mistake. First, they bother to consider all the elements that led to the conflict, diagnose the cause accurately, and apply the most matched response.

With good observation we can discern much about character and matching. Influential leadership means close, curious observation – before, during and after every interaction.

SUMMARY OF OBSERVING SKILLS

- Look at the other person often.
- Don't analyse what you see.
- Make conversations and emotional connection.
- Do your homework on who they are and what they want.
- Pause lots.
- Listen lots.
- Ask questions.
- Look at the interaction from an 'outsider' perspective.
- Watch out for the Drama Triangle.

9

REFLECTING

'Find all the good first. Judge by what has been done—not by omissions or mistakes. And look well into oneself! A life can well be spent correcting and improving one's own faults without bothering about others.'
– Edward Weston

REFLECTION – BEFORE, DURING, AND AFTER THE CONVERSATION

Reflection is like pauses – the notes unplayed. It is not part of the conversation, but it is what influential leaders do to have successful conversations.

An influential leader will reflect on what important conversations are coming up. During conversations, they will reflect on what is being said and observed, and afterwards they will consider the outcome and what is needed to further solidify agreement

REFLECTING – BEFORE THE CONVERSATION

How do you prepare for your big discussion? How do you prepare your counterpart? What do you know about them and how can you incorporate those bits of data into your conversation? You need to appear, as genuinely as possible, to be familiar to them. It is often those we have known for ages who are the very ones we take for granted or overlook. Do you really know them? Your influence will be diminished if you don't.

EXAMPLE – KNOW WHO YOU'RE TALKING TO

Dick Bass, son of a Texas oil baron, was known for going on ambitious mountain-climbing expeditions and talking about them, at length, to anyone within earshot, including a man who happened to be seated next to him on an airplane. For the duration of the cross-country flight, Bass went on about the treacherous peaks of McKinley and Everest and about the time he almost died in the Himalayas and his plan to climb Everest again. As they were about to land, Bass realised he hadn't properly introduced himself. 'That's okay,' the man said, extending his hand, 'I'm Neil Armstrong. Nice to meet you.'

With any important conversation, you want to create a positive expectancy about the outcome. This means you need to warm the other person up.

First, you need to reflect on the person and the context.

How do you feel about this person with whom you're about to speak? What's your expectation? If your expectations are good, how will you convey this? If you anticipate a negative response, why are you still having the conversation before you've changed your expectations? Are you ready for this conversation?

Second, you need to reflect on yourself.

Bias busters

Part of preparing yourself and the other person means spending more time on biases. Presenting identical information in different ways can lead to a change in the other person's response. This reframing, when offered in a matched way, can reduce an unconscious bias.

We have looked at the impact of the amygdala on our behaviour in contrast to the prefrontal cortex approach. In *Thinking, Fast And Slow,* Daniel Kahneman[20] refers to these as two types of thinking as **System One** and **System Two.**

System One is fast and intuitive, relying on mental shortcuts in thinking to navigate the world more efficiently. This is our amygdala at work, and is the source of our biases. By contrast, **System Two** is slow, and introduces deliberation and logic into our thinking. This is our prefrontal cortex at work.

Both systems impact how we make judgements, but the amygdala is in charge most of the time. We unconsciously 'prefer' System One because it is applied effortlessly. System One includes preferences we are born with, such as our desire to avoid losses and run from snakes, along with associations we learn, such as the answers to simple math equations.

Meanwhile, the prefrontal cortex requires attention in order to work – and attention is a limited resource. Thus, the deliberate, slow thinking of System Two is only deployed when we're paying attention to a specific problem. If our attention is distracted or threatened, System Two is disrupted.

Cognitive biases help us because if we had to carefully examine our options every single time we made a decision, we would quickly become overwhelmed. Consider deliberately weighing the pros and cons of each potential route to work every single day. Using the familiar route without thinking reduces stress and enables us to act quickly.

On the other hand, cognitive biases also lead to stereotyping, which can become ingrained from our exposure to our culture's biases and prejudices towards different races, religions, socioeconomic statuses, and other groups.

Personal motivations, social influence, emotions, and differences in our information processing capacities can all cause cognitive biases, which quietly insert themselves into our worldview.

Accepting many of our biases started aeons ago – look at how early and how subtly our gender bias is formed. In a research paper, *How preschoolers associate power with gender in male-female interactions,* the researchers asked 148 pre-school children to look at an image featuring two identical gender-neutral cartoon people, one adopting a dominant physical posture and one adopting a submissive posture. The children were told that one character was saying, 'You have to do everything I say!' and the other was saying, 'Okay! I will do what you want!'

They were then asked which character had power and which did not. Additionally, they were told that one of the figures was actually a man and the other a woman, and asked to identify which was which.

87.4 per cent of the children matched the dominant statement with the upright posture and the submissive posture with the submissive statement. And 75 per cent of those children who correctly identified the dominant party were also convinced the figure was male. These findings held across different cultures.

Researchers suggest there are over 100 biases, and it is useful to assemble them into manageable groupings. In reflecting, an influential leader makes themselves aware of as many of these biases as they can. Then, with that awareness, they reduce as many as possible.

Much of reducing bias in your leadership is done in preparation for the big discussion. Being flexible and alert to these pointers during the conversation itself is also very clever self-awareness.

Overload Biases

As discussed earlier, there is just too much information bombarding us. We have no choice but to filter almost all of it out. Our brain uses a few simple tricks to pick out the bits of information that are most likely going to be useful in some way.

Before and during the conversation, consider and adjust your filters.

People notice things that are already primed in memory or repeated often.

Notice what the other person triggers that is already primed for you. Note what buttons you have that might be pushed. Turn them off.

Bizarre, funny, visually-striking things stick out more than commonplace things. We tend to skip over information that we think is ordinary or expected.

Make note of the other person's bizarre and funny things and don't be overly impressed. Also note the ordinary, and be careful not to overlook it if it is important.

We love details that confirm our existing beliefs. We also tend to ignore details that contradict our beliefs.

Be clear about what you most strongly believe and be prepared to set that belief aside for a while. Spot your blind spot about what evidence you tend to ignore.

We notice flaws in others more easily than flaws in ourselves. It is very hard to be aware of this in the middle of the discussion, but try.

Meaning Biases

The world is very confusing, and we end up only seeing a tiny sliver of it. We take the sliver of information and fill in the gaps with stuff we think we already know. We find stories and patterns, which is how our brain reconstructs the world to feel complete and manageable inside our heads. We then assign meaning to these bits – the Ladder of Inference demonstrates how this happens.

We fill in characteristics from stereotypes, generalities, and prior histories whenever there are new specific instances or gaps in information. When we have partial information about a specific thing that belongs to a group of things we are pretty familiar with, our brain has no problem filling in the gaps with guesses. It then forgets which parts were real and which were made up.

Know what will push your buttons and remember the ways in which you tend to stereotype.

We react to things and people we're familiar with or fond of as better than things and people we aren't familiar with or fond of. *Do you like the other person or not? Be attuned either way.*

We simplify probabilities and numbers to make them easier to think about. Our subconscious mind is terrible at math and generally gets all kinds of things wrong about the likelihood of something happening if any data is missing.

Think about the ID profiles, and consider which aspects, such as Exaggerator/Understater or Rapid/Gradual, that enable this bias.

Share with the other person what you assume they're thinking.

Go Quickly Biases

Our amygdala causes us to act fast in the face of threat, so we can survive.

These days, this rarely saves our lives. Instead, it causes impulsive biases. As a result, we stamp down with controlling behaviour. We want quick, short-term solutions and resist the longer-term approach.

Be aware of your impatience and take time to pause and pick the moment. Let go of control. The more ego and importance you exhibit, the less you will be able to influence others.

The 'sunk cost' fallacy means we're motivated to complete things in which we've already invested time, money and energy. However, this can mean persevering or hanging on way past the time to let go.

Step back and review your progress objectively, and use external measures.

We also tend to choose the safest option. This relates to risk-taking and courage.

There is a difference between a simple solution that will work, and a quick fix that will unravel later. Know which is which.

Selection Biases

Because we only select certain things to remember, and worse, reinforce those selections after the event, we start to form rules about responding to situations, and don't actually consider each situation on its own merits.

These rules become our implicit associations, stereotypes, and prejudices.

Note what specifics you have clustered into a general pile and be sensitive to exceptions to the generalisation rule.

Carefully review your lists and look for what you have left out.

In Chapter One, we noted that we store memories differently based on the context of how they were experienced.

To unearth a context bias,
always consider the context in which you formed your memories.

By being aware of your possible biases, and noting your brain's strategies to solve them, you will ensure that you notice your biases more often.

Even the smartest person in a room can make the worst decision if they rely on intuition alone. Ultimately, the ability to identify and manage these cognitive biases will shape your decision-making and your capacity to be an influential leader.

REFLECTING – DURING THE CONVERSATION

During the conversation this means non-action. Not doing or saying anything, but mentally reflecting. Not playing the note. There are so many examples of how pauses and silence triggered a change for the better.

Reflection also involves a meta-communication about the conversation. You reflect on *what* has just been said, and *the way* it was said. You look at the scene from outside, as if you were viewing it through a window. What does it look like from this outside perspective? How does the conversation appear from outside?

Here are some suggestions for in-conversation reflection:

- Review your progress during the discussion – once in a while conduct a ten-second self-awareness audit. Are you missing some cues? Have you grasped their primary emotion? Are you feeling irritated, sad, or worried? Are you wondering if you might be wrong altogether?
- Use time out – do you need to step away? For a minute, half an hour, a day?
- Reflect out loud on your observations – this is referred to as meta-communication. It is greatly effective in minimising misunderstandings and maintaining trust. While very simple and easy, most of us never use meta-communication. It requires keen observation, and a willingness to be a little vulnerable – and perhaps wrong.

By taking a fragment of what the other person says and reflecting it onto them, they can they clarify their meaning and feel more connected.[21] For example:

It seems as though _____ is valuable to you.
It seems as though you do not like _____.
It seems as though you value _____.
It seems as though _____ makes it easier.
It seems as though you are reluctant to _____.

EXAMPLES – META-COMMUNICATION

You notice the other person is frowning and looking around.

'I see you are frowning and seem a little distracted. Is there a problem?'

You notice they are looking scared or uncomfortable.

'You seem uncomfortable. What's happening?'

You notice they interrupt.

'You want to say something. Please go ahead.'

You notice they seem distracted.

'Am I off track with this?'

REFLECTING AFTER THE CONVERSATION

Reflect on how you went.

I estimate that at least a quarter of important leadership conversations are ruined in the last two minutes. The accomplishments are undone by inadvertently reactivating the behaviour that caused the problem in the first place, such as, 'Great work John, so you will not be late to a meeting again!' Or, 'Let's stop there, Eva, I think you've got that anxiety beat.' Or, 'Good work Sara, no more shouting at people!' This instantly re-triggers the issue in their mind.

Rate yourself after each encounter. How did you go as an influential leader? Where were you on the amygdala to prefrontal cortex continuum?

Conduct your self-rating very stringently. My experience is that it is so easy to sneak back into amygdala leadership and drop the empathic prefrontal cortex leadership.

Amygdala leaders are reactive leaders who typically emphasise caution over action, self-protection over risk-taking, and individual frustration over collaboration. This leadership style is concerned with control. Amygdala leaders limit their influence and effectiveness, rather than increasing it.

The confusing reality is that amygdala leaders can achieve some excellent outcomes. Through fear and charisma, they can impel their teams to great heights. They often win battles, but not the war. They dominate minds, but do not win the hearts. They do what they believe is expected by their superiors – not necessarily what is right.

In contrast, prefrontal cortex leaders have won over their teams' hearts and minds. They have inspired a collaborative, sustainable 'can do' culture. They compose their own music, conduct it, and improvise if necessary. They maintain their skills and flexibly expand on them, modelling their strengths to encourage others.

Review and reflect on your own leadership performance with each new encounter.

YOUR ANNUAL EQ WORKOUT

EQ is central to empathy and influential leadership. So polish it up regularly.

Review your self-awareness skills

Review your body messages, such as sore neck, churning stomach, tired eyes, cold feet. What feeling goes with these signs? What started it? Why? Is there a recurring pattern, like the Drama Triangle? What are the early warning signs?

Identify and normalise the feelings

When you name your feelings, you activate your prefrontal cortex and help reframe the urge from your amygdala.

For example, admitting you are nervous to the audience you are speaking to paradoxically reduces your anxiety.

Labelling what you are feeling helps you and your counterpart respond appropriately and proportionately. Naming it makes you feel it and own it as being okay.

You need the correct label, and it needs to be nuanced. Does 'angry' mean killer rage, furious, upset, frustrated, or mildly annoyed? Does 'scared' mean uncomfortable, a little anxious, frightened, or terrified for your life? Does 'sad' mean mildly upset, tears, heartbreak, or years of depression? Does 'happy' mean ecstatic, delighted, pleased, or a slight smile?

Did your primary caretakers model tragedy when you got a bee sting, or did they take the view that 'it's nothing'? When you missed a goal in basketball, was there furious yelling or a mild 'no worries'? If you have absorbed some inappropriate or disproportionate feelings, you need to modify and reshape them.

Practise and expand the big four (anger, fear, sad, happy) into 40 nuanced gradations of each. Look up the range of feelings online. Ask for feedback from safe friends and colleagues. This ability to distinguish the finer grades of feelings will enable finer, more graduated leadership. Your matching of others will be even more seamless and sophisticated.

Even more importantly, you will take better care of yourself. Being able to distinguish a panic attack from pre-presentation nerves will help you get the appropriate support. Knowing the difference between being worn out and in need of a holiday is very different to being burnt out and needing hospitalisation.

VENT YOUR FEELINGS

There is the 'jet wind tunnel' way of expressing ourselves, and the 'light breeze' way of expressing ourselves. We tend to think any expression of emotion is going to be like the former and not the latter. Amygdala driven people are probably correct in this belief, but this is not true of people who engage their prefrontal cortex. Many people do not like to express their feelings, unless its happiness, and some people don't even like to express that one. Negative feelings in difficult conversations, where we need to give bad news, negative performance feedback, or even to fire someone, are never comfortable.

A while ago a CEO sent me one of his directors, whom he had just fired, to receive six months' paid career transition support. During my first session with the terminated director it became clear he had no idea he had been fired! He thought his boss had sent him to me for some remedial coaching.

There is discharging and ranting, or there is expressing feelings in order to resolve issues and to build relationships. Letting fly just feeds more bad feelings. Expressing feelings is on the list because bottling up our feelings does not work. Unresolved emotions will remain in your body and affect your life. We have seen how emotions leak out or display themselves in our body language, which is often even more dramatic if we try to suppress our emotions.

Manage your feelings

Some of us regulate our emotions with a glass of whisky. Others pause and count to ten, exercise, or go and sit in the park. We all use different and individual ways of managing our emotions.

Talking to yourself positively is good. Interestingly, using the third person is more helpful than using the first person. For example, saying, 'Graham, you are doing okay, you are just a bit anxious', works much better than saying, 'I am anxious'.

This is a nurturing parent/child dialogue, which is more comforting and agreeable. It is self-respecting empathy.

Reframing is another great regulator. Recalibrating your 9/10 anger to 5/10 anger, or deciding that your boss is having a bad day and you have done nothing wrong regulates your feeling.

SUSTAINING THE RESULT

Reflect on each encounter by following up your work and commitment building to cement your agreement with each person:
* Celebrate.
* Make the learning (yours and theirs) concrete.
* What was agreed or promised?
* How are you ensuring you or they follow up?
* Reinforce the commitment several times.
* Might any agreement need to be written down?

- Acknowledge their part in you getting what you want.
- Prepare for possible future collaboration together.

This is the last of our six VIP skills. Finally, we need to consolidate and confirm our new path of influential leadership.

SUMMARY OF REFLECTION SKILLS

- Rehearse in front of a mirror.
- Rehearse in front of a trusted audience.
- Do your homework before the conversation.
- Use meta-communication during your conversation.
- Consider what you know for sure versus what you have been taught.
- Examine and unearth your favourite biases and modify them.
- Ask yourself: what do you really know about the other person?
- Follow up after the conversation.
- Build future collaboration.

10

HOW TO KEEP ON BEING GOOD AT IT

'Pass on what you have learned. Strength, mastery, hmm ... but weakness, folly, failure, also. Yes, failure, most of all. The greatest teacher, failure is.'

– Yoda

NORMALISING THE NEW WAY

There are three major elements in embedding and remembering the things that you learn – repetition, rewards, and context.

These same three elements are the best way to help you to maintain the change from your old commitments to your new mindset of influence:

- Keep repeating the new behaviours, despite any small setbacks. Practise and engage the process even in small matters.
- Reward and recognise each small milestone and encourage others to acknowledge these as well. Recognise when you have done well. Pay attention to even small successes.

- Maintain the new context for change. Avoid or alter previous contexts where you tended to blame or sulk or dominate. Keep creating a new context where gratitude and respect can flourish. Make the new context your new normal.

ONGOING REVIEW AND MAINTENANCE

1. Revisit your two obstacles from Chapter One.

Is the new influence commitment comfortable now or are you still reverting to old ways? Where are you struggling – are there particular scenarios, particular people, or certain times of the day that present challenges to you? Can you change the scene, the people, and the time? If not, can you put more effort into changing yourself?

How is the fear of letting go and not being in control working out? Are little anxieties creeping back in? Have you noted some empathic conversations that did not work out which have caused self-doubt? Are you missing the sense of being in charge, or being in the know?

2. Review the gains and losses by making a list of them. Have a trusted advisor check the objectivity of your list. If the gains outweigh the losses then remember to be patient with yourself.

If the losses are greater than the gains, look at where you can make improvements.

3. Re-examine your Three Steps from Chapter Three. Is it still accurate? Do you need to change Step One behaviours or Step Two competing commitments? What about the big assumptions from Step Three? Are you still okay with these? Have other assumptions taken over or are your old assumptions reasserting themselves?

REVIEW YOUR INFLUENCE-SUPPORTING SKILLS

Matching

Are you doing it? Regularly? Naturally? What parts of matching are harder to remember? What needs some brushing up?

Influencing

Do you have your ID profile with you? Do you refer to it before every important conversation? Have you worked on reducing the potency of your two favourite dimensions? Do you assess the other person's ID before, during, and after the conversation? Are there some people and scenarios where you avoid using it? If so, why?

Respecting

Is your self-respect still strong? What are you doing to maintain it? How hard is it to respect others? How is the work on your biases?

Reframing

How often are you consciously setting a matched frame before, during, and after your conversations? Have you been developing a positive frame and reducing the negative frame? Is it tempting to be more direct and less subtle? Are you designing and using metaphors?

Observing

Do you pay attention to context, timing, and mood? If you measured your listening time versus your speaking time in your influential conversations in the last month, what would the ratio be?

Reflecting

Do you use reflecting during the conversation? Are you using metacommunication? Do you follow up on what was agreed or promised? Do you use the EQ checklist regularly?

An important final principle to reflect upon – a successful approach today may not be a successful approach tomorrow.

You might have worked out a very successful routine using this book only to find that suddenly it does not work. If this happens, it is due to the old saying, 'You can't step into the same river twice.' Adjust, be flexible and build a new routine. All the skills you need are here. Sometimes they may need a little rearranging.

Leadership is like this chart:

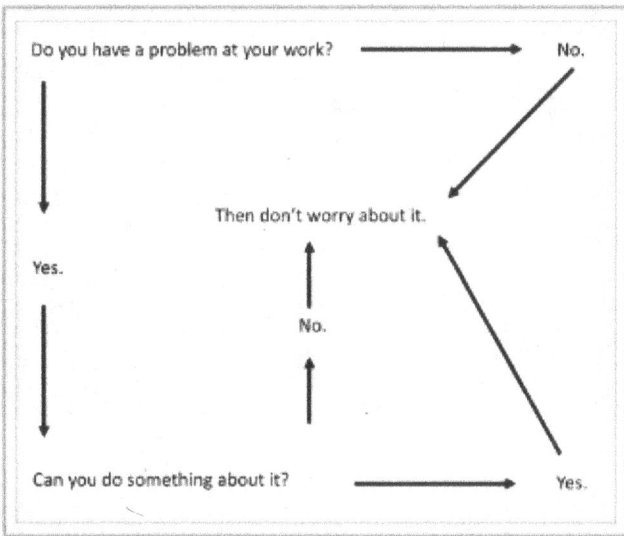

Finally, always remember the words of the Stoic philosopher, Seneca the Younger:

'If some obstacle arise, it is but like an intervening cloud, which floats beneath the sun but never prevails against it. You feel good not because the world is right, but your world is right because you feel good.'

Possible solutions to Nine Dot Problem:

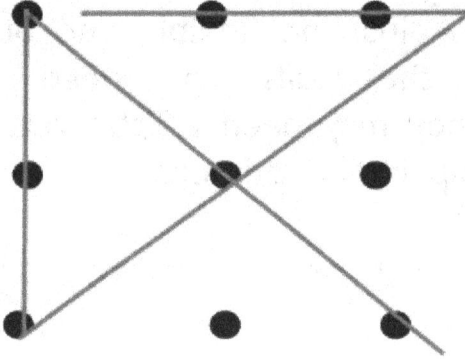

The Nine Dot Puzzle

(One of the many solutions to the puzzle)

ENDNOTES AND RECOMMENDED READING

[1]   Duhigg, C. 2012. *The Power of Habit: Why We Do What We Do in Life and Business*, Random House.

[2]   Davis, J Ph.D., Balda, M., Rock, D., McGinniss, P., Davachi, L. 2015. *The Science of Making Learning Stick: An Update to the AGES Model* (Vol.5) NeuroLeadership Institute.

[3]   Carlopio, J. & Andrewartha, G. 2012. *Developing Management skills: a comprehensive guide for leaders*, 5ed, Pearson, Sydney.

[4]   Schulz, Kathryn 2018. *Being Wrong: Adventures in the Margin of Error*http://amz n.asia/32pFJHK, and Brown, Brené. 2018, *Dare to Lead Brave Work. Tough Conversations*. Whole Hearts. Penguin.

[5]   Kerr, F. 2019. *The Art & Science of Looking up*—LOOKUP https://www.lookup.org.au > report.

[6]   Carlopio, J. & Andrewartha, G. 2012, *Developing Management skills: a comprehensive guide for leaders*, 5ed, Pearson, Sydney.

[7]   Cuddy, Amy. 2015, *Presence: Bringing Your Boldest Self to Your Biggest Challenges*, Little brown New York.

[8]   Carlopio, J. & Andrewartha, G. 2012, *Developing Management skills: a comprehensive guide for leaders*, 5ed, Pearson, Sydney.

[9]   Davies, E. *Reframing, metaphors, myths and fairy-tales*. Journal of Family Therapy, 10:83-92, 1988. Dennett, D. *Précis of The Intentional Stance. Behavioral and Brain Sciences*, 11: 495-546, 1988 and Watzlawick, P. (Ed.) *The invented reality*, New York: Norton, 1984.

[10]   Kegan, R. & Laskow Lahey, L. 2000. *How the way we talk can change the way we work: seven languages for transformation*. Jossey Bass, and Goulding, Mary McClure & Robert, 1979. *Changing Lives Through Redecision Therapy*, Brunner maezel

[11]   Goleman, D. 1996. *Emotional Intelligence: Why It Can Matter More Than IQ*, Bloomsbury.

[12]   Rock, D. 2009. *Your Brain at Work: Strategies for Overcoming Distraction, Regaining Focus, and Working Smarter All Day Long*. Harper Collins, New York.

339

[13]   Sapolski, R. 2017. *Behave: The Biology of Humans at Our Best and Worst,* Penguin Press.

[14]   Carlopio, J. & Andrewartha, G. 2012. *Developing Management skills: a comprehensive guide for leaders,* 5ed, Pearson, Sydney.

[15]   Cunningham, J. Barton. 2001. *Researching Organizational Values and Beliefs: The Echo Approach:* Lewin, K., Alex Bavelas and the Echo Approach. Praeger: *The Hidden Driver of Excellence,* Harper.

[16]   Goleman, D. 2013. *Focus: The Hidden Driver of Excellence,* Harper.

[17]   Senge, P. 1992. *The Fifth Discipline: The Art & Practice of the Learning Organisation,* Random House, Sydney.

[18]   Karpman, S. 1968. *Fairy tales and script drama analysis,* Transactional Analysis Bulletin.

[19]   Berne, E. 1973. *Games People Play: The Psychology of Human Relationships,* Penguin.

[20]   Kahneman, D. 2011. *Thinking, fast and slow,* Farrar, Straus & Giroux, New York.

[21]   Voss, C., Raz, T. 2018, *Never Split the Difference: Negotiating As If Your Life Depended On It,* HarperCollins.

REFERENCES

Many researchers and authors have stimulated my passion about the brain and leading and being a better human. This is just a few of my own idiosyncratic favourites you may care to read.

Kerr, Fiona. 2019, The Art & Science of Looking up—LOOKUP https://www.lookup.org.au > report

Damasio, Antonio. 2018, *The strange order of things*, Pantheon, New York.

Doidge, Norman. 2007, *The Brain That Changes Itself*, Viking, New York.

Cialdini, Robert. 2009, *Influence: The Psychology of Persuasion*, Collins Business Essentials, Boston.

Sharot, Tali. 2017, *The Influential Mind. What the brain reveals about our power to change others.* Little Brown, Great Britain1991.

Dennett, Daniel C. *Consciousness Explained*, Penguin Science.

Bianco, Margery Williams. 1922, *The Velveteen Rabbit*, Avon.

Chalmers, David J. 1995, *The Conscious Mind in Search of a Theory of a Conscious Experience.*

Block, Peter. 1993, *Stewardship,* Berrett-Koehler Publishers.

Watzlawick, P. (Ed.) 1984, *The invented reality,* Norton, New York.

Gottfredson, Ryan. 2020, *Success mindsets your keys to unlocking greater success in your life, work, and leadership.*

Deci, E.L., & Ryan, R.M. (2002). *Handbook of self-determination research.* University Rochester Press. *Honest Signals: How They Shape Our World* (MIT Press) Paperback – September 24, 2010 by Alex Pentland

Tversky, Amos; Kahneman, Daniel (1981). *The Framing of decisions and the psychology of choice,* Science. 211 (4481): 453–58. Bibcode:1981Sci ... 211..453T. doi:10.1126/science.7455683. PMID 7455683.

BACK COVER MATERIAL

As a forward-thinking leader, you are always looking at ways to improve your skills and techniques. You have a high level of knowledge about how to get the best from your people, and you are successful in achieving your goals.

Yet, in spite of your skills and knowledge, there are still breakdowns in communication, frustrating misunderstandings, and interpersonal difficulties you just can't seem to overcome. These barriers and roadblocks disrupt the smooth running of your business, wasting valuable time, energy, and money.

As a psychologist working with business leaders, Graham Andrewartha understands the reason these difficulties arise is because leaders bring their personal values, drivers, and biases into the workplace.

All too often, this key component of leadership development is not considered, placing leaders on the back foot with everything from culture to conflict resolution to creating cohesive teams.

In this book, Graham addresses these issues and teaches you how to:
- create positive mindset shifts
- develop empathic leadership
- recognise your influence style
- overcome limiting thought

- build trustworthy communication

This comprehensive guide to developing influential leadership is a must-read for any innovative leader wanting to take their skills, and their business, to the next level.

www.ingramcontent.com/pod-product-compliance
Lightning Source LLC
Chambersburg PA
CBHW011302210326
41599CB00036B/7098